street trees of seattle

street trees of seattle

SASQUATCH BOOKS
SEATTLE

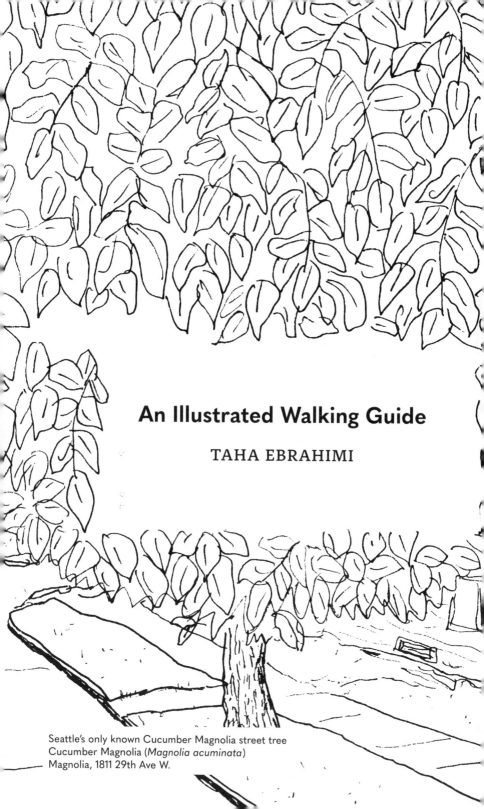

An Illustrated Walking Guide

TAHA EBRAHIMI

Seattle's only known Cucumber Magnolia street tree
Cucumber Magnolia (*Magnolia acuminata*)
Magnolia, 1811 29th Ave W.

She had never known silence . . . And scarcely knowing what she did, she stumbled forward and pressed the unfamiliar button, the one that opened the door of her cell.

E. M. FORSTER, *"The Machine Stops"*

Printed in China

SASQUATCH BOOKS with colophon is a registered trademark of Penguin Random House LLC

28 27 26 25 24   9 8 7 6 5 4 3 2 1

Editor: Jen Worick
Production editor: Isabella Hardie
Production designer: Tony Ong

Library of Congress Cataloging-in-Publication Data

Names: Ebrahimi, Taha, author, illustrator.
Title: Street trees of Seattle : an illustrated walking guide / Taha Ebrahimi.
Description: Seattle : Sasquatch Books, [2024] | Includes index. | Summary: "Using data visualization as a starting point, Taha Ebrahimi takes readers on a tour of existing trees throughout Seattle neighborhood and iconic parks through charming line drawings. In the process, she educates readers on the history of the trees and the city, and offers up drawings of leaves, trees, and leaflets as a charming but effective way to identify trees throughout the city"-- Provided by publisher.
Identifiers: LCCN 2023022101 (print) | LCCN 2023022102 (ebook) | ISBN 9781632174581 (paperback) | ISBN 9781632174598 (epub)
Subjects: LCSH: Trees in cities--Washington (State)--Seattle--Guidebooks. | Trees--Washington (State)--Seattle--Identification. | Seattle (Wash.)--Guidebooks. Classification: LCC SB435.52.W22 E27 2024 (print) | LCC SB435.52.W22 (ebook) | DDC 582.1609797/772--dc23/eng/20230725
LC record available at https://lccn.loc.gov/2023022101
LC ebook record available at https://lccn.loc.gov/2023022102

ISBN: 978-1-63217-458-1

Sasquatch Books
1325 Fourth Avenue, Suite 1025
Seattle, WA 98101

SasquatchBooks.com

MIX
Paper | Supporting responsible forestry
FSC® C008047
www.fsc.org

Table of Contents

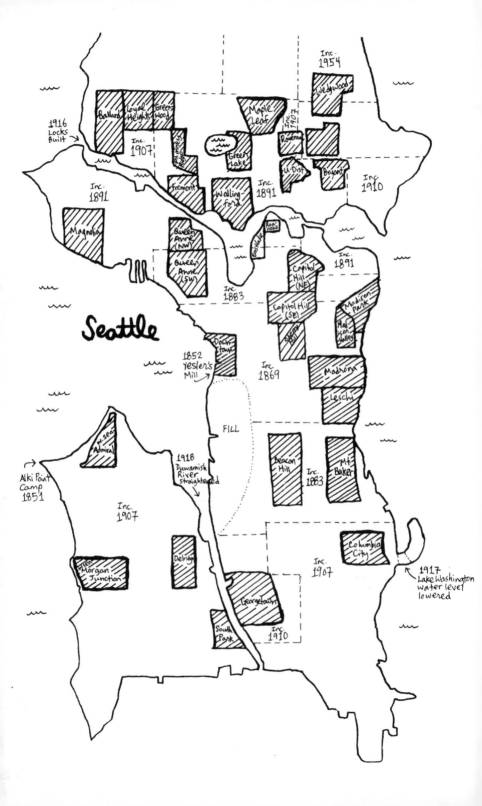

Seattle

1916 Locks Built

Ballard Loyal Heights Green Wood Maple Leaf Wedgwood

Inc. 1954

Inc. 1907 Green Lake Ravenna Inc. 1907

Phinney Ridge U-Dist Bryant

Inc. 1891 Fremont Walling-ford Inc. 1891 Inc. 1910

Magnolia Queen Anne (NW) Roosevelt Eastlake Capitol Hill (NE) Inc. 1891

Queen Anne (SW) Inc. 1883 Capitol Hill (SE) Madison Park

Green Lake Madison Valley

Downtown Madrona

1852 Yesler's Mill Inc. 1869 Leschi

FILL

Mt. Baker

Mt. sea Admiral Beacon Hill Inc. 1883

Alki Point Camp 1851 1918 Duwamish River straightened

Columbia City

Inc. 1907 Delridge Inc. 1907

Geo. Morgan Junction 1917 Lake Washington water level lowered

Georgetown

South Park Inc. 1910

Introduction

In the early part of the worldwide quarantine of 2020, while searching for new ways of being and feeling, I found myself taking epic walks and attempting to learn about trees. Since I was young, I equated horticultural knowledge with authority, the right to belong to a place, something I've always craved as a first-generation Seattleite. On my walks, I soon discovered that having a mission—to look for a specific tree species—forced me to develop a different relationship with time and to have unexpected conversations with familiar surroundings. It was as if a portal had opened, transforming the city I thought I already knew. The rejuvenating quality of "forest bathing"—the practice of immersing oneself in nature—gets a lot of attention, but what of our urban forest, the unsung "street tree"?

Seattle has over 730 different kinds of street trees across more than 150 different genera—one of the most diverse collections in the country, with a community of street trees more than double the diversity of the average community of street trees on the East Coast and triple the diversity of those in the Midwest. Street trees are commonly understood to be trees growing in a planting strip on a sidewalk (the city broadens the definition by also including trees in the public "right-of-way" or growing approximately 10 feet from the curb in the absence of sidewalks). In the 1970s, 40 percent of Seattle was shaded by our urban forest, but roughly 40 years later, that tree canopy had shrunk to 28 percent. Street trees make up nearly a quarter of the city's remaining tree cover, with the majority of our canopy existing on private residential property.

Eighty percent of the nation's population lives in urban areas and spends 93 percent of their time indoors but, during the global pandemic, walking became the only connection to the outdoors for many, and street trees were our closest contact to nature.

For me, identifying street trees is about making contact with a place. I had recently returned to Seattle after 15 years on the East Coast, and I found my hometown unrecognizable. Sense of place had not been considered in new development, and much of Seattle now appeared uniform, without identity or past. Street trees appeared to be one of the few anchors in these changing times, inextricably linked to location and public memory.

This was not the first time Seattle was made unrecognizable. Seattle is one of the fastest-growing US cities of the early 21st century, and while it's also one of the youngest, relatively speaking, it has undergone some of the most radical physical changes. Massive evergreens dominate our native forests, but 72 percent of our urban tree canopy is deciduous, and less than 5 percent is actually native to King County. Most of the trees we see today are nonnatives, and the oldest are 150 years *at most*.

The irony of the Emerald City in the Evergreen State is that its namesake greenery was largely clear-cut: In less than a month after arriving on the shores of West Seattle in 1851, the first European settlers felled and hauled 256 pilings of wood. Henry Yesler began operating a steam-powered sawmill the following year in present-day Pioneer Square, and the rest is history. The last original tree in the downtown area was logged in 1879. By 1910, Washington was the nation's largest lumber-producing state, and the industry employed almost two-thirds of the state's wage earners. In the present day, the only remaining stands of original, untouched old-growth trees in Seattle are in parts of Schmitz and Seward Parks (with isolated specimens here and there). Solastalgia itself—the distress caused by losing one's environmental sense of place—is perhaps our strongest tie to understanding our shared history.

Since the Garden of Eden, trees have been central to our stories. Trees were some of the first places of worship in many spiritualities and religions, far before temples. People have planted trees in cities for over 400 years, but the concept of planting trees en masse expressly for public spaces began only in the 16th century—in France, where imposing Lombardy poplars made popular by private Italian Renaissance gardens were planted in rows along a national system of royal post roads, creating the perception of a uniform identity across separate regions. The use of the word *boulevard* to mean "a tree-lined street" can be traced to one specific location in Paris atop the remains of the city's ramparts or "bulwarks" near the old Porte Saint-Antoine gate in the 4th arrondissement. Planting trees reflected power, authority, and resources. (In response, during the French Revolution, mobs sometimes protested against aristocratic rule by planting trees in public squares.)

In colonial America, a haphazard street tree style developed as early as 1686, in which individual homeowners would plant trees in front of their houses regardless of whatever their neighbors may have planted. The result was a hodgepodge of random trees on a single street, an appropriate reflection of the American ethos of independence and individuality. This lack of organized tree planting was seen as a failing of American cities in comparison to European cities, where street trees were the responsibility of municipalities. But, as the United States was formed and the nation grew, so did its concept of street trees. Washington, DC, the first town to be designed by the federal government, was planned by French-born architect Pierre L'Enfant in 1791, with avenues of street trees modeled after those leading to the palace at Versailles—and it was one of Thomas Jefferson's first undertakings as president to have Lombardy poplars planted along Pennsylvania Avenue in 1803. In 1872, that city would become the first in the United States to implement a comprehensive street tree-planting program, the same year Arbor Day was established.

Around the same time, a belief was developing that proper places created proper behaviors and that nature encouraged moral virtue and civic pride in otherwise wretched urban populations, and so the model of a green "City Beautiful" gained popularity in the wake of vaunted public green spaces like New York City's Central Park. Planting street trees took on a class agenda. It was an act of public good defined by the wealthy for the benefit of the poor. Throughout the second half of the 19th century, as the practice of street tree planting spread across the world, trees often came as part of a package that included Western forms of paving, transportation, sanitation, and education.

Seattle's own urban street tree planting began in earnest in the 1900s, fueled by the desire to be a major city following in the steps of the City Beautiful movement. Surges in street tree planting coincided with events that brought visitors to the city, including the Alaska-Yukon-Pacific Exposition in 1909 and, later, the Seattle World's Fair in 1962. The city's official street tree data goes back to 1950 with just 800 trees listed by 1966. Ironically, most street trees were added thanks to the construction of federally funded highways. In 1968, one year before Interstate 5 was completed in Washington, bonds were issued for "arterial-street beautification," which allowed for 17,000 street trees to be added throughout the 1970s (although about 300–400 were vandalized each year, according to the city arborist).

Seattle's relationship with individual tree species and street trees over the decades reveals quirky reports of civic engagement and tangled intentions (detailed in the following pages). In 1976, a citizen went as far as suing Seattle City Light over what the Seattle Times described as the city's "inaction concerning the plight of street trees," resulting in a task force being appointed to work on city ordinances regarding trees. "Street trees do more to enhance the city than any piece of sculpture," the plaintiff argued. "You need to preserve what is culturally strong in a nation, or devastation can result."

Almost 50 years later, with legal protections still hotly debated, only one thing is clear: our associations with the humble street tree are uniquely complex. The urban forest occupies a weird place between our concept of what is private and public. Street trees are a reflection of society's evolving ambiguities and the way we view them has always been as much about humans as the trees themselves.

Street Trees of Seattle is based on a data set published in 2020 by the Seattle Department of Transportation's Urban Forestry team, which includes seven decades of information about more than 170,000 publicly and privately maintained trees considered to be in the public "right-of-way." The trees curated for this book represent a moment in time—a living, disintegrating capsule. Street trees live shorter, tougher lives than their wilder counterparts, and as we press forward, these trees will grow and change, and some will inevitably vanish.

A 1991 survey of street trees in 20 cities established that 13 years was the average life span of an inner-city street tree, but the "average" city is not Seattle. Most of the trees curated for this book are far older. Studies show that large trees that have taken decades to grow provide more impact on human well-being than younger trees—and retaining and maintaining the big trees we already have is cheaper and more efficient at reducing excess atmospheric carbon than any man-made solution. In the time I was researching this book since the pandemic first began, we lost several notable street trees, including Seattle's widest (by trunk diameter) maple, ash, and black locust. The iconic flowering cherry street trees that once lined Pike St. welcoming visitors to the oldest consistently operating public market in the country were unceremoniously cut down to make way for a newly designed sidewalk. The absence of a tree is as much a part of this story as its existence.

Whatever may come, the Greek physician Hippocrates used to prescribe: "If you are in a bad mood, go for a walk. If you are still in a bad mood, go for another walk." Street tree walks can be taken in any season and any weather (although they often happen in the winter, in rain). Go alone or with others. Pick one tree or an entire genus. Clues are everywhere. Take notes. In this period of uncertainty, trees comfort and ground, reminding us that we are intertwined with the past, and the future was and has always been unknown.

Data and Methodology

When I first started learning about trees, I relied on two books: David Allen Sibley's *The Sibley Guide to Trees* and Arthur Lee Jacobson's *Trees of Seattle*. One provided detailed illustrations, and the other provided specific addresses for local trees by species. I originally began drawing maps, tree locations, and species characteristics out of pure necessity, in an effort to combine the different types of information for each walk into a single efficient page I could easily carry with me. As one year of the pandemic turned into two, my curiosity grew, and I found the Department of Transportation's public data on right-of-way trees.

Data alone cannot tell the story. Only humans can do that. The more I worked with the city's data set, the more I noticed issues. For example, the information provided for "date planted" reveals only when the tree was recorded, not the actual age of the tree. (Many of the trees that are listed as having been planted in the 1990s were recorded as part of a large-scale street tree survey: the trees had already existed for years.) "Data was collected on paper sheets, and dots were placed on paper maps; the data was only later digitized," current City of Seattle arborist Nolan Rundquist explained to me. "We can't accurately record the planting date in our inventory using our field data collection application [because] the software we use won't accept a date prior to January 1, 1950."

In certain situations, I noticed the city data set was incomplete and had left out some street trees, like the cherry plums planted on my parents' street in Bryant. Also, while there is a field in the data set to indicate the "site type" and whether the trees are in sidewalk planting strips or in private yards overhanging the "right-of-way," this is inconsistently recorded, and since I wanted to focus on traditional street trees in planting strips, this meant painstaking manual validation. Because of the sheer scope and limited timeline, I used Google Maps Street

View more than once to ensure that specific street trees were even still there before I visited them in person (sometimes, even those images were old, and I would arrive to find a tree gone anyway).

I limit my maps to primarily one tree genus per neighborhood, because I found that on my own walks, narrowing the scope of what I was looking for helped me better absorb and retain nuanced details. In an age of what feels like relentless and overwhelming information, less is more memorable. The slight variations between species force one to slow down and observe in new ways. For those who prefer big and old trees, I've also included each neighborhood's "notable" street trees across different genera. There are deliberately no designed paths on these maps; the routes are up to those participating. Each walk is unique and thus unrepeatable, a pilgrimage or spell.

I am neither an arborist nor an illustrator, but draw everything by hand because I'm a visual learner; the *physical act* of drawing or writing is how I've always learned. Things I read on-screen fade into the ether as if never read at all. The ubiquity of the typewritten word means many in younger generations can't read cursive or handwriting, so consider this a swan song, a love letter to love letters. Still, while the resulting maps are imperfect analog drawings, they certainly would not have been possible without the technology behind them.

To determine which neighborhoods would be included and which neighborhood would focus on which tree genera, and to identify which specific trees would be highlighted, I used a variety of analysis tools including the free data visualization software Tableau Public (full transparency: I work there), and yes, even classic Excel spreadsheets.

The presence of certain street trees is what determined which neighborhoods were included in this book and which were not. This immediately reduced the possibilities—only a few neighborhoods had a wide enough range of maple species within walking distance of each other, and only one neighborhood had a monkey puzzle street tree. I also looked for the first-recorded street trees within a genus or species and those with the widest trunks, and if a neighborhood had one of these notable trees, I sometimes started there. As specific neighborhoods and tree genera were checked off the list, the task grew harder.

Neighborhoods like Capitol Hill, Wallingford, and Queen Anne were repeatedly the best neighborhoods for finding multiple different tree species, forcing me to make tough choices based on complex and imperfect tiers of logic. Other neighborhoods were seemingly bereft of street trees, closely matching economic indicators. (In Seattle, our wealthiest neighborhoods consistently have more street trees than the lowest income areas.) Sometimes, the deciding factor for tree inclusion was simply that I liked the look of a specific tree specimen, or because the tree was on a walkable street. Other times, I decided to leave entire tree genera out, like alder and hornbeam. Where possible, I favored featuring trees in planting strips rather than those in the right-of-way often in private yards.

In total, I've included more than 50 types of tree genera across 33 neighborhoods. (Trees in the additional parks and cemeteries I've included were not sourced from the street tree data set, as trees in green spaces owned by Seattle Parks and Recreation and on private property are not considered to be in the right-of-way.) On every field walk, I lamented the street trees I did not include.

In the publicly available data set I analyzed, trunk diameter was the most reliable and complete category of information that was consistently recorded. There were fields for tree height and overall tree grow span including branches, but these were not always filled in. As a result, I relied primarily on trunk diameter to identify which trees were noteworthy, but it should also be pointed out that comparison based on trunk diameter is not exact, since the trees were validated in person by the city on irregular and staggered schedules, rather than at one point in time. Furthermore, the standard method to measure trunk diameter, known as "diameter at breast height" or DBH, has its own inherent bias since "breast height" depends on the person (in the United States, it has been established that 4.5 feet is considered breast height, but internationally, it is fiercely contested). To use this information to compare or rank trees is fraught, but I do it anyway because it's what we have. The bias toward focusing on trunk diameter is reflective of the limitations data can impose. Certainly, other trees are noteworthy for other aspects, many of which are overlooked in my selections.

This is a reminder that data is flawed from the *very moment* it is collected: it consists of only what can be measured, which is by nature only the superficial. The nature of data is a dual trap. In the specific case of this book, not only are there overlooked trees but the trees that are included take on incommensurate importance; the information collected takes highest priority simply because it exists, creating a bias toward trunk diameter, an emphasis on an arbitrary arborary aspect. It reminded me that data analysts and researchers are similarly expected to use data as their starting point, but such analysis inevitably underestimates the bias that is implicit in collecting and processing data, discounting the intangibles of lived experience. Data is many things but, most of all, data is dangerous, because it lends a false sense of objectivity and truth, as if it illuminates the totality of a picture.

This is why data can have unintended impacts. In the year I worked on this book, the City of Seattle defined an "exceptional tree" worthy of municipal protections as a tree with a diameter of 30 inches or more. But some trees are just naturally skinny even when they are very old, like crape myrtle and goldenchain, which rarely ever exceed a 30-inch trunk. Meanwhile, poplars and giant sequoias grow rapidly and are our widest trees in trunk diameter because they are naturally big trees, not necessarily more in need of protection. Trunk diameter might be a useful data point when comparing within species (*this* is even debatable), but it's largely irrelevant when comparing the worth of a tree across different genera of varying average sizes. Yet this is how the city's street tree data has been used, and this is how the city's policy was originally shaped. (Watch your back, crape myrtle!)

As I walked the neighborhoods of Seattle to validate the trees behind the data points in person, I regularly noticed other trees that were destination-worthy for various reasons—trees hunched in strange shapes, trees in beautiful locations, trees that evoked memories and witnessed history. In Leschi, I saw an English maple with an abnormal growth sheathing its trunk, making it appear cinched at its waist. A man walking his dog at the time stopped to comment about how unusual the tree was and how everyone in the neighborhood used it as a landmark. It would be ridiculous *not* to include this tree in a list of noteworthy street trees, yet it had not turned up in any of my analyses because it did not rank high in any of the categories of information that had been collected in the city's data; the growth was too far up the trunk to be counted as part of the measurement of its trunk diameter. In fact, the tree didn't rank highly no matter how I sorted the fields. If I had not taken a physical walk in the neighborhood and seen the entire tree in person—and if I had only been at my desk limiting my analysis to just the data (as much analysis is often done)—I would have missed this landmark tree.

When strangers stopped me on my tree validation walks to ask what I was doing, I watched their perplexed expressions as they processed what may have seemed like an absurdist project in an absurd time, but to me, it did not feel any less so than the hundred inane and irrelevant things I regularly did in context of the COVID-19 pandemic. As vaccines were rolled out in the spring of 2021 and the world began to open up again, I started to make contact with real-life tree experts, like Arthur Lee Jacobson. While I was an interloper using a data set to shortcut finding the city's notable trees, he had completed his own book about Seattle's trees in the 1980s without any data—by literally walking or biking the streets of the city. He generously offered to go on tree data validation walks with me, and with his in-person help, it became slowly clear that the penultimate comedy of my project was that the city's data wasn't always right (corrections are noted in the following pages). Of the roughly 600 trees validated for this book, 20 percent had been originally misidentified. Jacobson shared that much of the street tree data from the 1990s was actually collected by volunteers with incomplete knowledge, rendering an unknown quantity of the inventory unreliable. This was another warning of how treacherous insights derived from data analysis can be when divorced from the physical data points. From what I understand, Seattle's tree inventory is better than most cities, but even here one needed to always assume a significant margin of error.

According to ecological engineer Nadina Galle, many cities across the United States and around the world lack proper tree inventories, which could otherwise be used as the foundation for urban forest management to ensure tree species diversity and optimal tree distribution. "If you were to have municipalities laying down bridges, roads or any other part of our civil infrastructure without any other information or data associated with it, nobody would tolerate that, because we know the infrastructure would crumble," Galle told me. "For a long time, we saw street trees as a way to beautify our cities rather than the critical infrastructure that we now know."

The trees haven't changed, but we are learning new things every day about how they do more than just make a street look pretty. One square mile of urban forest can release the daily oxygen requirement for roughly 10,000 people, and there is still so much we don't understand about the relationship between trees and human health, such as why an area's loss of mature trees is associated with additional cardiovascular-related human deaths and illnesses of the lower respiratory system, or why hospital patients who can see trees from their windows are discharged earlier. The fallacy of "big data" is that real insight requires human scale, and there is no substitute. Data is still mostly only "directional" *even at its best.*

All that being said, while this tree data may be flawed, it was still enough for me to generally *see* the urban forest. To obsess about the individual data points and discount the value of the information as a whole would have been to lose the forest for the trees. Deeper analysis, of course, requires a level of intimate understanding that must take place beyond the numbers. My hope is that this book will take you there, helping you make contact with the urban forest, to know the stories that came before us and to connect with a sense of place that data by itself can never capture.

BLOOM TIMES &

| JAN. | FEB. | MAR. | APR. | MAY | JUN. |

ACER
- SILVER MAPLE
- RED MAPLE
- BIGLEAF MAPLE

PRUNUS
- CHERRY PLUM
- PEACH
- ALMOND
- WEEPING HIGAN CHERRY
- YOSHINO CHERRY
- JAPANESE HILL CHERRY
- COMMON PLUM
- 'HOSOKAWA-NIOI' CHERRY
- 'SHIROTAE' CHERRY
- 'KWANZAN' CHERRY
- MAZZARD CHERRY
- BIRCHBARK CHERRY

MALUS
- APPLE
- CRABAPPLE

MAGNOLIA
- KOBUS, STAR & HYBRID MAGNOLIA
- SAUCER MAGNOLIA
- YELLOW MAGNOLIA
- GALAXY MAGNOLIA

CORNUS
- PACIFIC DOGWOOD
- EASTERN

AESCULUS
- HORSE CHESTNUT
- REDFLOWER
- YELLOW BUCKEYE

ARBUTUS
- PACIFIC MADRONA

CATALPA +

EVERYTHING ELSE
- PEAR
- YEW
- ELM ------- ELM SEEDS
- OVENS WATTLE
- HOLLY
- REDBUD
- GOLDENCHAIN
- BLACK LOCUST
- QUINCE
- HAWTHORN
- MANNA ASH
- GINKGO
- EUCALYPTUS
- PALM
- TAMARISK

FRUIT TIMES

JUL.	AUG.	SEP.	OCT.	NOV.	DEC.

CHERRY PLUMS
PEACH (mostly fruitless street trees)
ALMONDS (mostly nutless kinds here)

PLUMS

CHERRIES

APPLES

CRABAPPLES

2nd bloom, SAUCER MAGNOLIA

CUCUMBER MAGNOLIA

EVERGREEN MAGNOLIA

SWEETBAY MAGNOLIA

DOGWOOD

2nd bloom, PACIFIC DOGWOOD
PACIFIC DOGWOOD FRUIT (inedible)

KOUSA DOGWOOD

KOUSA DOGWOOD FRUIT (inedible)

HORSE CHESTNUT CONKERS (inedible)

STRAWBERRY TREE

MADRONA BERRIES (inedible)
STRAWBERRY TREE BERRIES (inedible)

NORTHERN CATALPA

SOUTHERN CATALPA

CHITALPA

PEARS (most street trees fruitless)

YEW BERRIES (inedible)

HOLLY BERRIES (inedible)

QUINCE FRUIT

HAWTHORN "HAWS"

GINKGO

PERSIMMON

PERSIMMON FRUIT

LINDENS (Bigleaf first)

TULIP TREE

TREE OF HEAVEN

CHESTNUT

CHESTNUT NUTS

SILK TREE

CHINESE SCHOLAR TREE

LOQUAT FRUIT

LOQUAT

CRAPE MYRTLE

WALNUTS

ACORNS (inedible)

BUTTERNUTS

Notes on Using this Guide

Whenever the term "widest diameter" is used, it refers to trunk diameter at breast height (DBH). Whenever the term "district" is used, it refers to Seattle's seven Council Districts.

Whenever an entry is noted as being "not illustrated," it means the tree does not appear on its associated neighborhood map. Please also note that the maps and illustrations in this book are not to scale or exact.

When visiting these trees in person, remember some are on private property, so please don't trespass or disturb in any way.

Exercise caution. Between 1995 and 2007, one report found 407 deaths related to "tree failures" in the United States, with Washington ranking second highest. Be aware on windy and also hot days when, believe it or not, a phenomenon known as sudden branch drop (SBD) can occur.

The Trees by Neighborhood

Yoshino cherry (*Prunus × yedoensis*)
7733 33rd Ave. NW

BALLARD Cherry

In the early 20th century, Seattle was the "cherry tree gateway" for America—all flowering cherry trees arrived from Japan first in the ports of the Emerald City, including the first 2,000 famous flowering cherries of Washington, DC, which initially arrived in the Pacific Northwest by ship in 1909 before traveling by refrigerated railcar to their East Coast destination.

Over the decades, thousands more cherry trees would come through Seattle, with gifts sent by Japan every year from 1929 to 1932. People of Japanese descent made up Seattle's largest minority in this period until World War II, when it was reported that many of the flowering cherries in the city were cut down around the same time the Japanese community was forcibly removed from their homes in Washington and incarcerated in isolated military camps. Although more than one-third of the incarcerated never returned, in one of the first gestures of postwar healing, Japan gifted Seattle a new batch of cherry trees in 1950 to replace those that had been destroyed. The blooms, which last for only a few weeks, remind us of the delicate and ephemeral nature of the most beautiful things.

The genus Prunus *includes cherry, cherry plum, apricot, peach, and almond trees, and it makes up the second-most abundant type of street tree in Seattle, with more than 28,000 trees overall responsible for removing four million pounds of carbon dioxide from our atmosphere each year. District 6, which includes Ballard, has the most* Prunus *street trees in the city.*

"the tree of hope"

PRUNUS
DECIDUOUS
Total: 28,668 (17% of all right-of-way trees in Seattle)

Birchbark Cherry
(PRUNUS SERRULA)
Max Height: 60'+

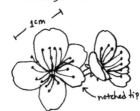

- shiny peeling red bark
- white flowers (late April)
- 5 petals
- flowers in clusters of 2-4
- tiny cherries (inedible)

notched tip
1cm

FROM W. CHINA

① 2653 NW 56th St., incorrectly recorded in the city's data as wild black cherry

Cherry Plum
(PRUNUS CERASIFERA)
Max Height: 50'

- purplish leaves
- pink flowers (most in March with some hybrids blooming mid-April)
- 5 petals
- flowers borne singly from branch
- cherry plums (June)

round tip
1cm

FROM MIDDLE EAST

② 6719 27th Ave. NW, a pair recorded in the city's data as 'Blireiana purple-leafed' plum (a hybrid with 10-petal flowers) but are instead likely 'Newport' —the latest cherry plum to bloom

'Kwanzan' flowering Cherry
(PRUNUS 'KWANZAN')
Max Height: 50'+

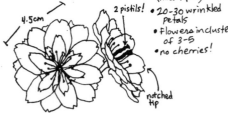

2 pistils!

- pink flowers (mid-April)
- 20-30 wrinkled petals
- flowers in clusters of 3-5
- no cherries!

notched tip
4.5cm

FROM JAPAN

③ 6101 34th Ave. NW

'Hosokawa-nioi' flowering Cherry
(PRUNUS 'HOSOKAWA-NIOI')
Max Height: 50'

- white flowers, later with pink centers; fragrant
- 5 petals
- flowers in clusters of 3-7 on long stems
- tiny cherries (June) (inedible)

notched tip
3-4cm

FROM JAPAN

④ City's "lost" Hosokawa-nioi cherry street trees: 7502 Earl Ave. NW (on NW 75th St.) a little known Japanese cultivar which sold for decades in the West as 'Shirotae' (Seattle claims to have none)

4

Ballard

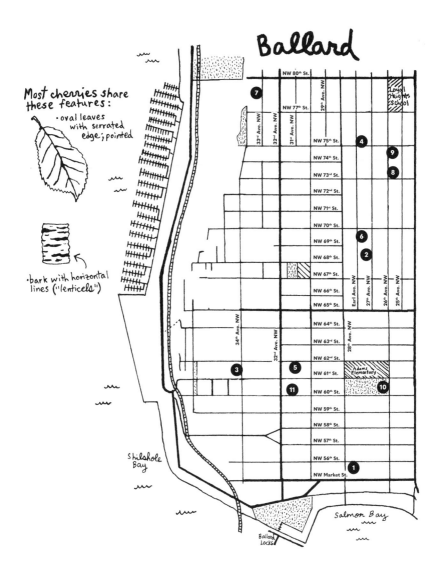

Most cherries share these features:
- oval leaves with serrated edge; pointed
- bark with horizontal lines ("lenticels")

MAzzard Cherry
(PRUNUS AVIUM)
Max Height: 110'

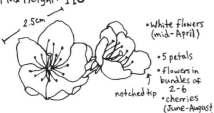

- White flowers (mid-April)
- 5 petals
- flowers in bundles of 2-6
- notched tip
- cherries (June-August)

FROM EUROPE, N. AFRICA, MIDDLE EAST

⑤ Seattle's first-recorded cherry tree in the public right-of-way: 3033 NW 62nd St., in private yard hanging over sidewalk; listed in city's data on January 1, 1950, the date scientists have established as the cut-off for accurate radiocarbon dating (estimates after this date are now calibrated for additional carbon in the atmosphere due to nuclear weapons testing)

'Hosokawa-nioi' flowering cherry (*Prunus* 'Hosokawa-nioi)
7502 Earl Ave. NW (on NW 75th St.)

Yoshino Cherry
(PRUNUS X YEDOENSIS)
Max Height: 56'

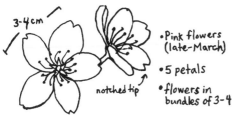

3-4 cm

- Pink flowers (late-March)
- 5 petals
- flowers in bundles of 3-4

notched tip

FROM JAPAN

⑥ 6733 Earl Ave. NW, lining the street, recorded in the city's data as only "Cherry/Plum/Laurel"

⑦ **Tied for third- and fourth-widest diameter cherry street trees in Seattle: 7712, 7716, 7722 and 7733 33rd Ave. NW:** lining the street is the largest concentration of the city's widest diameter cherry street trees (listed incorrectly in city's data as 'Kwanzan' Japanese flowering cherry)

Also see:

- **Possibly the oldest miniature "dwarf" street tree in Seattle (also 14th-widest diameter peach street tree in city):** Ravenna (6533 20th Ave. NE)
- **Widest diameter almond street tree in Seattle:** Phinney Ridge (162 NW 62nd St.)
- **Widest- and second-widest diameter cherry street trees in Seattle:** Cherry Hill, Japanese Hill Cherry (300 and 312 21st Ave.)
- **Tied for third-widest diameter cherry street tree in city:** Ravenna, Yoshino cherry (1315 NE 70th St.)
- **Widest diameter mazzard cherry street tree in Seattle (also tied as fifth-widest-diameter cherry street tree in Seattle overall):** Phinney Ridge, mazzard cherry (6216 Evanston Ave. N.)
- **Second-widest diameter mazzard cherry street tree in Seattle:** Maple Leaf (819 NE 84th St.)
- **Seattle's only *Prunus* Heritage Tree street trees:** Bryant, single-flower weeping Higan cherry (5230 35th Ave. NE)
- **City's most popular cherry trees:** University of Washington Quad, Yoshino cherry (Pierce Ln., University of Washington)
- **Widest diameter Yoshino cherry street tree in Bryant:** 5539 39th Ave. NE
- **Highest concentration of 'Akebono' Yoshino cherry street trees in Seattle:** Capitol Hill (926 21st Ave. E.)
- **University District's only 'Shirotae' flowering cherry street tree:** 4306 University Way NE
- **Widest Akebono and 'Kwanzan' cherry street trees in Columbia City:** 5040 49th Ave. S. and 3952 S. Hudson St.

BALLARD
other notable street trees:

Cider Gum Eucalyptus
(EUCALYPTUS GUNNII)

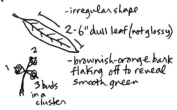

-irregular shape

2-6" dull leaf (not glossy)

-brownish-orange bark flaking off to reveal smooth green

3 buds in a cluster

8 Tied for second-widest diameter eucalyptus street tree in the city: 7338 26th Ave. NW; listed in city's data only as *"Eucalyptus sp."*

Deodar Cedar
(CEDRUS DEODARA)

- dark, furrowed bark

1-2" needles on spurs in clusters

4" upright, round cone

9 Third-widest and tied for fifth-widest diameter cedar street tree in Seattle: 7348 26th Ave. NW, a pair

London Plane
(PLATANUS X ACERIFOLIA)

3-5 lobes

two seed balls per stalk

-swollen, burly trunk

-mottled, scaly bark

10 Second- and third-widest diameter plane street tree in Seattle: 2644 NW 60th St., a pair bordering Ballard Playground's east side on 26th Ave. NW; these trees are also the widest Heritage Trees in the city

Sawara Cypress
(CHAMAECYPARIS PISIFERA)

- stringy bark; open and sparse

-prickly, curling foliage, yellowish and soft

1/4" round <u>wrinkly</u> cone

11 Second-widest diameter false cypress street tree in Seattle: 3048 NW 60th St.; listed incorrectly in city's data as a Lawson cypress

London plane (*Platanus x acerifolia*)
2644 NW 60th St.

BEACON HILL
holly

Ninety percent of English holly sold in the United States is grown in the Pacific Northwest, with the first-recorded English holly planting having taken place in 1891, only two years after Washington became a state. But the story of holly in Seattle truly begins in 1927, when Lillian McEwan (wife of the owner of Ballard's Seattle Cedar Lumber Manufacturing Company) founded the Washington State Society for the Conservation of Wild Flowers and Tree Planting and began her inexplicable personal mission to plant so much English holly that Washington could one day become "the Holly State."

Over the next decade, thousands of seedlings and trees were planted, mostly by children enlisted by McEwan. Seattle Girl Scouts planted 1,500 small holly trees in Seward Park at a 1928 Arbor Day picnic. In 1930, another 1,000 children attended the annual planting event. Incidentally, even though McEwan's stated goal was to "protect and rescue native plants and trees," English holly was not native and, in fact, it was invasive, nearly engulfing Seward Park. Today, the King County Noxious Weed Board classifies holly as a "weed of concern," and the story of Seattle's English holly has become a cautionary tale of unexpected consequences.

Seattle has roughly 540 holly right-of-way trees, and District 2, which includes Beacon Hill, is one of three districts with the least. Developed in part by early 20th-century prisoners, Jefferson Park is where planes used to land before the city's first airfield in 1928.

English holly (*Ilex aquifolium*)
1512 S. Bayview St.

Holly

"the tree of domestic happiness"
ILEX
EVERGREEN
Total: 542 (0.3% of all right-of-way trees in Seattle)

Beacon Hill

S. Plum St.
(9)

(11) S. Hill St.

(5)

S. Walker St.

(4) S. Walker St.

16th Ave. S.
17th Ave. S.
18th Ave. S.
19th Ave. S.
20th Ave. S.
21st Ave. S.
22nd Ave. S.
23rd Ave. S.

(3) S. Bayview St.

El Centro

S. Waite St. (13)

S. Lander St.

Light Rail Stop
S. McClellan St.

S. Forest St.

S. Stevens St.

(8) (12)

S. Winthrop St.

(6)

S. Hanford St.

(2)

Beacon Ave. S.

S. Horton St.
(7)

Lafayette Ave. S.

S. Hinds St.

(1)

Alamo Pls.

S. Spokane St.
(10)

Jefferson Park

12

English Holly
(ILEX AQUIFOLIUM)
Max Height: 100'

3½" stiff, glossy leaf (some prickly)

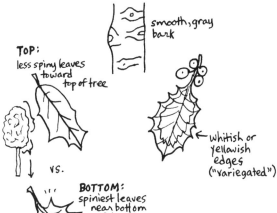

¼" females make red berries, in clusters (also greenish and whitish)

smooth, gray bark

TOP: less spiny leaves toward top of tree

vs.

BOTTOM: spiniest leaves near bottom of tree to protect it

whitish or yellowish edges ("variegated")

FROM EUROPE, N. AFRICA, W. ASIA

1 3307 Lafayette Ave. S., an 'Argentea Marginata,' with cream-edged leaves

2 2001 S. Hanford St. (on 20th Ave. S.)

3 **Widest diameter holly street tree in District 2:** S. 1512 S. Bayview St., a female tree with berries

4 2208 16th Ave. S.

5 1409 S. Hill St.

-tiny flowers (April-May)-

female ♀   male ♂

green oval in center

stamens (little "antenna")

Also see:

- **Tied as widest diameter English holly street tree in Seattle:** Cherry Hill (1129 15th Ave.); University District (1802 NE 55th St.); *Not illustrated:* Phinney Ridge (108 N. 55th St.)
- **Second-widest diameter English holly street tree in Seattle:** University District (1802 NE 55th St.)
- **Third-widest diameter English holly street tree in Seattle:** Greenwood (8103 6th Ave. NW)
- **Seattle's widest diameter holly tree overall:** Volunteer Park, Capitol Hill (1247 15th Ave. E.)

BEACON HILL

other notable street trees:

Chinese Windmill Palm
(TRACHYCARPUS FORTUNEI)

6 **Only palm street tree in District 2 that is listed in the city's data as an unknown species:** 3117 22nd Ave., a male with an uncharacteristically smooth trunk unlike other Chinese windmill palms that have shaggy trunks; one tree expert suggested the mysteriously bare trunk could be due to "humans desiring to turn it into a coconut palm" while others disagree

English Midland Hawthorn ⑦
(CRATAEGUS LAEVIGATA)
Max Height: 40'

Third-widest diameter hawthorn street tree in Seattle: 3230 Lafayette Ave. S.

- similar bark/trunk as common Hawthorn

2" leaf, less lobed than common Hawthorn

May to June: pinkish-red flowers, often with 10+ petals, very fragrant (blooms earlier than common Hawthorn)

½" red fruit, 2-3 seeds

European Beech
(FAGUS SYLVATICA)

First-recorded beech street tree in Seattle: Beacon Hill Ave. S., south of S. Stevens St.; while the other beeches lining this street were listed in the city's data in 1991, two on the east side (3014 and 3020 Beacon Ave. S.) were listed on January 1, 1965, the same day the SS *Catala* (which had been used in 1962 as a floating "boatel" for visitors of Seattle's World's Fair) ran aground in Ocean Shores during a storm; cleanup of the wreck—which contained about 25,000 gallons of fuel oil—was only completed four decades later, in 2007 ⑧

- spreading tree with smooth gray bark

3" oval leaf with wavy edge (green)

prickly fruit nut

Evergreen Magnolia
(MAGNOLIA GRANDIFLORA)

Seattle's fourth-widest diameter magnolia street tree: in traffic circle at S. Plum St. and 19th Ave. S. ⑨

6-11" glossy, leathery leaf with brown fuzz underneath

- white flowers late-May

Evergreen magnolia (*Magnolia grandiflora*)
S. Plum St. traffic circle

Ginkgo
(GINKGO BILOBA)

10 Seattle's widest diameter Ginkgo street tree: 1756 S. Spokane St., female

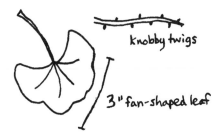

knobby twigs

3" fan-shaped leaf

Lawson Cypress
(CHAMAECYPARIS LAWSONIA)

11 Fifth-widest diameter false cypress street tree in Seattle: 1602 S. Hill St. (on 16th Ave. S.)

- fibrous, reddish bark
- scaly, flattened fans of foliage

$\top$
$\frac{3}{8}$" seed cone
$\bot$

Strawberry Tree
(ARBUTUS UNEDO)

12 Only strawberry tree street tree in Beacon Hill: 1915 S. Stevens St.

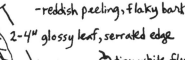

- reddish peeling, flaky bark

2-4" glossy leaf, serrated edge

tiny white flower clusters (winter)

$\top$
1" red spiky fruit (October)
$\bot$

Common Orchard Apple
(MALUS X DOMESTICA)

13 Widest orchard apple street tree in District 2: 2508 19th Ave. S.

- spreading tree; tangled branches

3" toothed leaf

$\top$
5"+
$\bot$

1¼" pink flowers (March to April)

BRYANT
monkey Puzzle Tree

Ties between the monkey puzzle tree and the Pacific Northwest go back as far as the tree's introduction outside its native Chile. In 1792, Captain George Vancouver led an expedition to explore North America's Pacific coast, and on the voyage back to Great Britain, he and his crew stopped in Chile, where they were served edible seeds from an unusual looking tree. The ship's botanist, Archibald Menzies, pocketed some of the seeds and grew them during the trip home, which is how he introduced five young saplings to Britain in 1795, along with the crew's other findings from the Pacific Northwest territory, forever associating the monkey puzzle with this region.

In Seattle, this odd evergreen was featured in the *Seattle Daily Times* in 1925, when a listing advertised a 10-foot-high tree that could be purchased for $5 (about $85 today). By 1960, the cost of a monkey puzzle tree in Seattle was advertised as $9.95 (or $100 today). Then the organizers of the 1962 World's Fair decided to hand out *free* monkey puzzle saplings—which is when many of the trees you see in the city today were planted. By 1975, a scarcity of seeds was reported across the city.

There is only one monkey puzzle street tree in a planting strip left in the entire city of Seattle, and it is located in Bryant, a neighborhood named after Bryant School, which itself was named after the 19th-century poet and New York Evening Post *editor William Cullen Bryant (who, unlike the monkey puzzle tree, had not even a slight connection to Seattle).*

Monkey puzzle (*Araucaria araucana*)
5538 39th Ave. NE

monkey puzzle
"the tree of protection"

ARAUCARIA ARAUCANA
Max Height : 77'
Total : 14 (0.008% of all right-of-way trees in Seattle) with only one in a planting strip

EVERGREEN (FROM S. CHILIE, SW ARGENTINA)

1½" sharp, triangular "leaves"

7" upright cone ♀

rounded crown

spiny branches

straight trunk, gray and fissured

1. Seattle's only monkey puzzle street tree in a planting strip: 5538 39th Ave. NE

2. Calvary Cemetery: 5041 35th Ave. NE, three large trees near the west side of the central square pathway

Bryant

other notable street trees:

Paper Birch
(BETULA PAPYRIFERA)

- white bark peeling at edges

3½" oval leaf
(double-toothed)
5-10 pairs of veins

- pendent catkins

❸ Calvary Cemetery: 5041 35th Ave. NE, massive trees near the east side of the central square pathway

American Persimmon
(DIOSPYROS VIRGINIANA)

- crooked trunk; bark broken into checkers

4½" oval leaf with wavy edge

- orange fruit (remaining through winter)
- ripe: October

❹ Seventh- and eighth-widest persimmon street trees in Seattle: 4501 NE 60th St. (on 45th Ave. NE)

Tulip Tree
(LIRIODENDRON TULIPIFERA)

5" leaf with 4 lobes

- upswept branches
- upright green/orange flowers (June)

❺ Eighth-widest tulip tree street tree in Seattle: 3311 NE 60th St., Heritage Trees lining the east border of Bryant School

Weeping Higan Cherry
(PRUNUS X SUBHIRTELLA 'PENDULA')

Max Height: 80'

- late March bloom
- white/pale pink flowers
- weeping branches
- 5 petals
- 3-4 flowers per cluster

❻ Seattle's only *Prunus* Heritage Tree street trees: 5230 35th Ave. NE, a pair

Yoshino Cherry
(PRUNUS X YEDOENSIS)

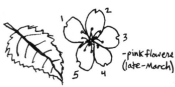

- pink flowers (late-March)

❼ Widest Yoshino cherry street tree in Bryant (third-widest in District 4): 5539 39th Ave. NE, several

Bigleaf maple (*Acer macrophyllum*)
5506 6th Ave. S (Georgetown)

European Chestnut (*Castanea sativa*)
5922 41st Ave. SW (West Seattle)

Giant sequoia (*Sequoiadendron giganteum*)
1104 17th Ave. E. (on E. Prospect St.)

Northeast
CAPITOL HILL
Redwood

Despite its name, the dawn redwood is unlike other redwoods and conifers: it loses its needles each year. Originally from China, dawn redwoods were introduced to Seattle only in 1948. Coast redwoods and giant sequoias have been in this region much longer.

Native to coastal Northern California and Oregon, coast redwoods date back as far as 150 million years, to the Jurassic period. They are the tallest trees on the planet, but 95 percent of old-growth redwoods have been logged. Many of the original buildings of the late 1800s in San Francisco were built from their lumber.

The other redwood—the giant sequoia—is known to live up to 3,000 years and is one of the longest-living organisms on the planet, as well as one of the largest trees by sheer mass, storing at least three times more carbon above ground than other forests. The drought of the 2010s left many of Seattle's giant sequoias stressed from lack of water, exhibiting symptoms of dehydration. Though sequoias usually die by falling under their own weight, recently scientists have seen some decline so rapidly that they expire while still standing.

There are 73 coast redwood, 102 giant sequoia, and 117 dawn redwood street trees in Seattle. Capitol Hill is home to the first-recorded and the widest diameter redwood street trees, as well as a coast redwood that is the city's tallest nonnative tree, planted in the early 1900s in a grove by the abandoned boulevard in Interlaken Park (once the city's first paved bicycle trail).

Redwood
"the tree of wisdom"

Coast Redwood
(SEQUOIA SEMPERVIRENS)
Max Height: 370'
(from coasts of N. California to SW Oregon)

1" needles in feathery, flat sprays

- yellowish pollen cones at twig tips

- reddish, fibrous, ridged bark

1" cone

EVERGREEN • Total: 73 trees (0.04% of all Seattle right-of-way trees)

1 Seattle's widest diameter coast redwood in data set (when including right-of-way trees): 2105 E. Highland Dr., yard corner at 21st Ave. E.

2 Second-widest diameter coast redwood street tree in a planting strip in Seattle: 611 16th Ave. E.

3 Tallest nonnative tree in city: Interlaken Park: 2451 Delmar Dr. E., directly across from a grove by the stairs beside old road

Dawn Redwood
(METASEQUOIA GLYPTOSTROBOIDES)
Max Height: 125'
(from China)

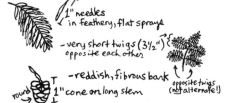

1" needles in feathery, flat sprays

- very short twigs (3½") opposite each other

- reddish, fibrous bark

round → 1" cone on long stem

opposite twigs (not alternate!)

DECIDUOUS • Total: 117 trees (0.06% of all Seattle right-of-way trees)

4 17th Ave. E., north of E. Mercer St.: 1624 E. Mercer St., a very small one missing from the city's records

5 925 14th Ave. E.

Giant Sequoia
(SEQUOIADENDRON GIGANTEUM)
Max Height: 274'
(from N. California Sierra Nevada mountains)

- cord-like twigs with tiny, sharp scale-like "leaves"

- reddish, fibrous, ridged bark

2½" cone

EVERGREEN • TOTAL: 102 TREES (0.06% of all Seattle right-of-way trees)

6 Widest diameter giant sequoia street tree in Seattle: 1104 17th Ave. E., on E. Prospect St., a massive leaning specimen

7 Sixth-widest diameter giant sequoia street tree in Seattle: 753 18th Ave. E. on E. Aloha St.

8 Volunteer Park: 1247 15th Ave. E., east of the museum, middle of lawn

9 Lake View Cemetery: 1554 15th Ave. E., tree at top of hill south of circular path, planted in 1906 at the grave of Catherine Maynard (wife of David "Doc" Maynard who named Seattle)

Capitol Hill

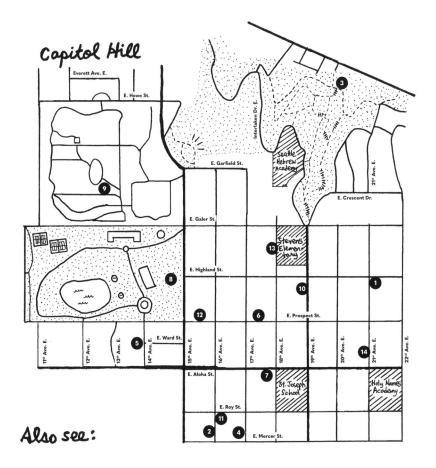

Also see:

- **Widest diameter coast redwood street tree in a planting strip in Seattle:** West Seattle, Admiral (1627 Sunset Ave. SW)
- **Third-widest diameter coast redwood street tree in Seattle (when including right-of-way trees):** Madrona (3909 E. Howell St.)
- **First-recorded and fourth-widest diameter coast redwood street tree in Seattle (when including right-of-way trees):** *Not illustrated:* West Seattle, Fauntleroy (9677 47th Ave. SW)
- **Sixth-widest diameter coast redwood street tree in Seattle (when including right-of-way trees):** South Park (8320 10th Ave. S.)
- **Third-widest diameter coast redwood street tree in a planting strip in Seattle:** West Seattle, Morgan Junction (5956 37th Ave. SW)
- **Widest diameter giant sequoia in Seattle (when including right-of-way trees):** West Seattle, Morgan Junction (6531 40th Ave. SW)
- **First-recorded giant sequoia tree (when including right-of-way trees):** Mount Baker (3212 Hunter Blvd. S.)
- **Downtown's widest diameter giant sequoia street tree (out of only two):** triangle at 4th Ave., Stewart St. & Olive Way
- **Second-widest diameter dawn redwood street trees in Seattle:** Loyal Heights (2501 NW 80th St.)

other notable street trees:

Common Horse Chestnut
(AESCULUS HIPPOCASTANUM)

7 leaflets (14" total)

—white flowers in 10" clusters with yellow/red markings (May bloom)

10 Second-widest diameter horse chestnut street tree in Seattle: 1151 19th Ave. E.

Chinese Juniper
(JUNIPERIS CHINENSIS)
Max Height: 80'

small berries at tips ↗

scaly foliage in dense clumps and pointed sprays creating irregular, zig-zaggy shape

11 Widest diameter juniper street tree in Seattle: 620 16th Ave. E.

Western Red Cedar
(THUJA PLICATA)

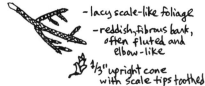

— lacy scale-like foliage

— reddish, fibrous bark, often fluted and elbow-like

1/3" upright cone with scale tips toothed

12 Second-recorded western red cedar street tree in Seattle: 1508 E. Prospect St.; three western red cedars listed on September 11, 1950, the same day President Harry S. Truman signed NSC-68, a National Security Council recommendation to contain the expansion of the Soviet Union

Hybrid Black Walnut
(JUGLANS NIGRA x
JUGLANS HINDSII)

17-19 leaflets

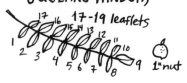

1" nut

13 Third-widest diameter walnut street tree in Seattle: 1223 18th Ave. E.; listed incorrectly as a white ash

'Akebono'' Yoshino Cherry
(PRUNUS X YEDOENSIS 'AKEBONO')

- pink flowers (late March/ early-April)
- 5 petals

14 Lining both sides of street with widest diameter at 926 21st Ave. E. (a 1920s cultivar from California with pinker flowers than Yoshino)

Bigleaf maple (*Acer macrophyllum*)
920 19th Ave. E.

southeast
CAPITOL HILL
Maple

Maples were Seattle's first known street trees, planted in 1859 by settlers Henry and Sarah Yesler in front of their home in present-day Pioneer Square, on the north side of James Street between First Avenue and Second Avenue. They are no longer there but are ignominiously memorialized in drawings depicting the 1882 lynching of three white men, who were hanged from the trees by an angry vigilante mob. King County's sheriff at the time, Louis Wykoff, died of a heart attack when he and his deputies were unable to stop the violence. Children later dared each other to climb the maples and cut pieces of the remaining rope. Reportedly, the crossbeam strung between the trees that the men were hanged on was left up for several years as a cautionary tale.

By the turn of the 20th century, maples were the most commonly planted tree in Seattle. The native bigleaf maple species made up over 90 percent of the city's maples until its massive sidewalk-splitting size rendered it illegal to plant as a street tree by city ordinance. Today, maples are still the most abundant street tree in Seattle, with more than 36,000 responsible for removing six million pounds of carbon dioxide from our atmosphere each year, except now the dominant species is the Japanese maple.

District 3, where Capitol Hill is located, is home to one of the city's widest diameter maple street trees, as well as the biggest variety of different mature maple species in the city. Nearly 35 percent of the neighborhood is shaded by right-of-way trees, one of the highest rates of canopy coverage in Seattle.

Maple

"the tree of reserve"
ACER
DECIDUOUS
Total: 36,978 (22% of all right-of-way trees in Seattle)

Bigleaf Maple
(ACER MACROPHYLLUM)
Max Height: 158'

12" stalk — 5 deep lobes
-ridged bark with thick twigs
9"+ leaf (blunt teeth)
-yellow/brown fall color
1¾ winged fruit, greenish and hanging in clusters

FROM SW CANADA TO CALIFORNIA

1 Tied as widest diameter maple street tree in Seattle: 920 19th Ave. E.

2 17th Ave. E. & Harrison St.: NE corner has an eight-trunked specimen that isn't ranked as notable in the city's data

3 Second-widest diameter bigleaf maple street tree in this part of Capitol Hill: 1700 17th Ave., north of Olive

English Maple
(ACER CAMPASTRE)
Max Height: 110'

2½"
-twigs with "corky" ridges
3-5 lobed leaf with rounded teeth
1½" fruit with 180° wings

FROM EUROPE, N. AFRICA, W. ASIA

4 Widest diameter English maple street tree in Capitol Hill: E. Harrison & Federal Ave. E.: center traffic circle

Japanese Maple
(ACER PALMATUM)
Max Height: 50'

7 (5-9) lobes
-contorted trunk and branches
3" leaf (toothed)
¾" winged fruit, spreading

FROM SW CHINA, KOREA, JAPAN

5 Widest diameter Japanese maple street tree in Capitol Hill: 323 16th Ave. E.

Norway Maple
(ACER PLATANOIDES)
Max Height: 137'

5 lobes (broad)
-furrowed bark, twigs opposite
5" leaf, slightly curling edges
-mostly yellow fall color
1¾ greenish winged fruit; spreading

FROM EUROPE, W. ASIA

6 Widest diameter Norway maple street tree in Capitol Hill: 713 13th Ave. E.

Capitol Hill

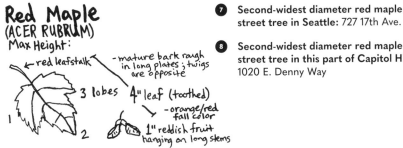

Map labels (streets):
E. Prospect St.
E. Aloha St.
E. Roy St.
E. Mercer St.
E. Republican St.
E. Harrison St.
E. Thomas St.
E. John St.
E. Ward St.
E. Aloha St.
E. Valley St.
E. Denny Way
E. Howell St.
E. Olive St.

10th Ave. E.
Federal Ave. E.
11th Ave. E.
12th Ave. E.
13th Ave. E.
14th Ave. E.
15th Ave. E.
16th Ave. E.
17th Ave. E.
18th Ave. E.
19th Ave. E.
20th Ave. E.

Lowell Elementary
St. Joseph School

= School
= Park, P-Patch
= Light Rail Station

FROM EAST AND CENTRAL N. AMERICA

Red Maple
(ACER RUBRUM)
Max Height:

← red leafstalk
- mature bark rough in long plates; twigs are opposite
3 lobes   4" leaf (toothed)
- orange/red fall color
1" reddish fruit hanging on long stems

7 Second-widest diameter red maple street tree in Seattle: 727 17th Ave. E.

8 Second-widest diameter red maple street tree in this part of Capitol Hill: 1020 E. Denny Way

33

Silver Maple
(ACER SACCHARINUM)
Max Height: 138'

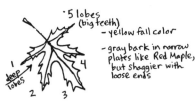

· 5 lobes
(big teeth)
— yellow fall color

— gray bark in narrow plates like Red Maple, but shaggier with loose ends

deep lobes

1

2   3   4

├──── 6½" leaf; ──┤
silvery underside

1¾" winged fruit, greenish and spreading wide

Sugar Maple
(ACER SACCHARUM)
Max Height: 151'

5 lobes   (center lobe parallel)
— few teeth

— yellow/orange/red neon autumn color

— gray-brown bark, furrowed and plated

1

2   3   4

├───── 5" leaf ─────┤
with drooping edges

1" winged fruit; 90° or less (greenish wings turn brown)

FROM EAST AND CENTRAL N. AMERICA

9 Widest diameter silver maple street tree in Seattle: 434 16th Ave. E.

10 Second-widest diameter silver maple street tree in this part of Capitol Hill: 1920 E John St., incorrectly listed in city's data as sugar maple

FROM EAST AND CENTRAL N. AMERICA

11 Widest diameter sugar maple street tree in Seattle: 615 17th Ave. E.

12 Second-widest diameter sugar maple street tree in this part of Capitol Hill: a pair at 225 14th Ave. E.

Also see:

- **Tied as widest diameter maple street tree in Seattle:** *Not illustrated:* Northgate, bigleaf maple (11045 15th Ave. NE); University District/Ravenna, bigleaf maple (5723 17th Ave. NE); *Not illustrated:* Sand Point, bigleaf maple (12003 Bartlett Ave. NE)
- **Second-widest diameter maple street tree in Seattle:** Georgetown, bigleaf maple (5506 6th Ave. S.)
- **Tied as third-widest diameter maples street tree in Seattle:** SW Queen Anne, bigleaf maple (1224 3rd Ave. W.); *Not illustrated:* Cherry Hill, bigleaf maple (2202 E. Olive St.)

CAPITOL HILL (Southeast)
other notable street trees:

American Elm
(ULMUS AMERICANA)

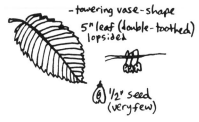

- towering vase-shape
5" leaf (double-toothed) lopsided
1/2" seed (very few)

13 Tied as eighth-widest elm street tree in Seattle: 1110 E. John St. (on 11th Ave. E.)

Atlas Cedar
(CEDRUS ATLANTICA)

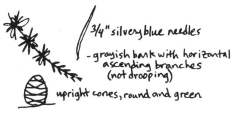

3/4" silvery blue needles

- grayish bark with horizontal ascending branches (not drooping)

upright cones, round and green

14 First-recorded cedar street tree in Seattle (also tied for fifth-widest diameter cedar street tree in the city): 1405 E. John St. (on E. John Ct. across mini park); listed September 18, 1950, the same day the US National Security Resources Board presented its long-awaited "master blueprint" for building the nation's civil defenses; today, the state of Washington is home to the world's third-largest nuclear arsenal

Chinese Scholar Tree
(SOPHORA JAPONICA)
Max Height: 100'

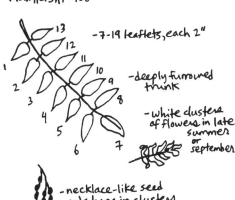

- 7-19 leaflets, each 2"

- deeply furrowed trunk

- white clusters of flowers in late summer or september

- necklace-like seed pods hang in clusters

15 Widest diameter Chinese scholar tree in the state of Washington: Cal Anderson Park, NW corner across from the light-rail station (1635 11th Ave.); not a street tree but included in city's data because it is a Heritage Tree

European Beech
(FAGUS SYLVATICA)

3" leaf with wavy edges

– smooth gray bark like elephant skin

16 Fourth- and fifth-widest diameter beech street trees in Seattle: 510 17th Ave. E.

Deodar Cedar
(CEDRUS DEODARA)

1-2" needles clustered on spurs

– grayish black bark

♀ 4" round, green cone

17 Fourth-widest diameter cedar street tree in Seattle: 202 18th Ave. E. (on E. John St.)

Green Ash
(FRAXINUS PENNSYLVANICA)
Max Height: 145'

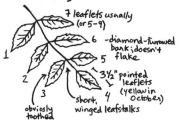

7 leaflets usually (or 5-9)

– diamond-furrowed bark; doesn't flake

3½" pointed leaflets (yellow in October)

obviously toothed

short, winged leafstalks

18 Tied as fourth- and sixth-widest diameter ash street trees in Seattle: 131 13th Ave. E., a row

London Plane
(PLATANUS X ACERIFOLIA)

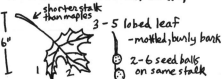

shorter stalk than maples

3 - 5 lobed leaf

– mottled, burly bark

2-6 seed balls on same stalk

6"

20 Third-widest diameter plane street tree in Seattle: 734 16th Ave. E.

Manna Ash
(FRAXINUS ORNUS)

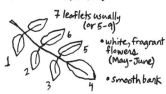

7 leaflets usually (or 5-9)

• white, fragrant flowers (May-June)

• smooth bark

21 Widest diameter manna ash street tree in Seattle (also tied as sixth-widest diameter ash street tree in city overall): 224 14th Ave. E.

Balleana White Poplar
(POPULUS ALBA 'PYRAMIDALIS')

22 Eighth-widest poplar street tree in Seattle: 115 18th Ave. E., a pair

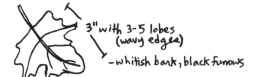

3" with 3-5 lobes (wavy edges)

— whitish bark, black furrows

Lombardy Poplar
(POPULUS NIGRA 'ITALICA')

23 Widest diameter poplar street tree in Seattle: 907 14th Ave. E., a pair (with widest sporting massive burls)

serrated, heart-shaped leaf

⊢ 3" ⊣

Tree of Heaven
(AILANTHUS ALTISSIMA)
Max Height: 102'

24" leaf total with many leaflets, each with a few teeth near base (red when young)

- gray bark with interlacing ridges and very thick twigs

- yellow-green flowers at twig tips in mid-summer

- papery seeds hang in clusters

A Deeper Dig

The tree of heaven was brought to the United States in the 1700s from China and had a brief period of popularity as a street tree in the middle decades of the 19th century due to its hardiness and resistance to inchworm infestations. Given its name purportedly because of its ability "to grow towards the heavens very quickly," at one point in New York City "ailanthus mania" led to the replacement of many healthy horse chestnuts and lindens, eliciting public outcry. When it was discovered that the tree also produced a bad odor, one New York newspaper editorial suggested that "every man who has an ailanthus tree in his neighborhood, should make it his duty to destroy it." Today, there are roughly only 60 tree of heaven street trees in Seattle, and their days may be numbered, as they are the preferred host of the crop-devastating spotted lanternfly, which was first found in the United States in Pennsylvania in 2014 and has been moving west, despite federal quarantines.

Tulip Tree
(LIRIODENDRON TULIPIFERA)

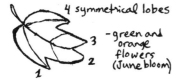

4 symmetrical lobes

- green and orange flowers (June bloom)

25 Fifth-widest diameter tulip tree street tree in Seattle (also a Heritage Tree): 747 16th Ave. E., with sidewalk customized around it

Strawberry Tree
(ARBUTUS UNEDO)

- reddish, shredding bark
- 2-4" green, glossy leaf

3/4" spiky red fruit (October to December)

- white "urn"-shaped flowers; tiny, in bushels (fragrant) (September - December)

2"

26 Widest diameter strawberry tree street tree in Seattle: 1018 E. Thomas St. (on Federal Ave. E.), melded to a white birch street tree

Tamarisk
(TAMARIX PARVIFLORA)
Max Height: 44'

- lopsided tree with scaly haze-like twigs
- 2 1/2" pink spikes of flowers (blooms late-May to early June)
- shredding, scaly bark

27 Seattle's only known tamarisk street tree: 1732 16th Ave. (on E. Howell St.); listed in the city's data as "Unknown"

CAPITOL HILL

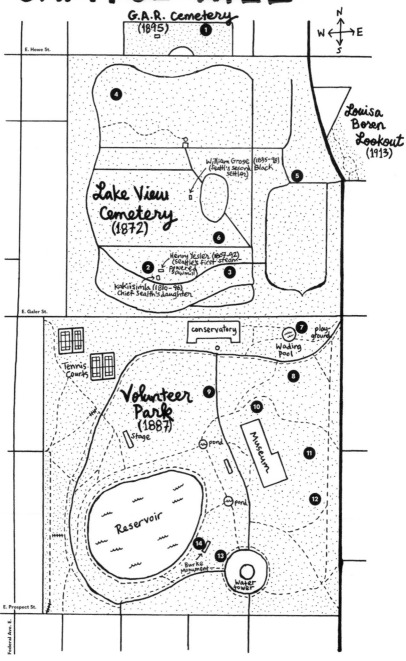

G.A.R. Cemetery (1895) **1**

E. Howe St.

N
W — E
S

4

Louisa Boren Lookout (1913)

William Grose (1835-98) (Seattle's second settler) Block

5

Lake View Cemetery (1872)

6

Henry Yesler (1807-92) (Seattle's first steam-powered sawmill) **3**

2

Kakiisimla (1810-96) Chief Sealth's daughter

E. Galer St.

conservatory

7 playground

Wading Pool

8

Tennis Courts

Volunteer Park (1887) **9**

stage

10

Museum

11

pond

12

pond

Reservoir

14

13

Burke Monument

Water Tower

E. Prospect St.

Federal Ave. E.

Grand Army of the Republic (G.A.R.) Cemetery • 1895

① **Hybrid elm (Ulmus x hollandica)**
Everett Ave. E., east of E. 12th Ave.: nine elms lining northern border

Lake View Cemetery (1554 15th Ave E.) • 1872

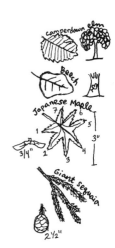

② **Camperdown elm (Ulmus glabra 'Camperdownii')**
Southwest part of cemetery, near Phinney plot

③ **Copper beech (Fagus sylvatica f. purpurea)**
South side along path, growing over tombstones

④ **European beech (Fagus sylvatica)**
Northwest part of cemetery, near steps

⑤ **Japanese maple (Acer palmatum)**
At the entrance where the road forks northward

⑥ **Giant sequoia (Sequoiadendron giganteum)**
At the top of the hill at Lake View's highest point

Volunteer Park (1247 15th Ave. E.) • 1887

⑦ **Cluster pine (Pinus pinaster)**
Northeast of wading pool; old sign grown into it

⑧ **Austrian pine (Pinus nigra)**
Four in a line across the road south of the wading pool

⑨ **Western red cedar (Thuja plicata)**
A grove of elbow-y trees south of the conservatory

⑩ **Copper beech (Fagus sylvatica f. purpurea)**
North of the museum is Seattle's widest beech tree

⑪ **Giant sequoia (Sequoiadendron giganteum)**
Two giants east of the museum

⑫ **English holly (Ilex aquifolium)**
Southeast of museum is city's widest holly, a berryless male

⑬ **Norway spruce (Picea abies)**
A grove west of water tower

⑭ **Weeping Higan cherry (Prunus subhirtella 'Pendula')**
East of the reservoir near the Burke monument

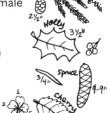

CHERRY HILL
Ash

The ash tree is one of the most sacred trees in Germanic paganism. In Norse mythology, an immense ash tree known as Yggdrasil, or the "World Tree," was at the center of the cosmos, with its trunk reaching up to the heavens, its boughs spread over nine realms, and its roots reaching down into the underworld. Seattle City Light didn't care much about any of this in 1958, when it cut down a 40-year-old ash street tree on West Blaine Street, west of Queen Anne Avenue. The homeowner filed a claim against the city, stating: "Instead of an old house with a beautiful shade tree, we now have just an old house." Payment of $185 was made to the homeowner by the city for what it claimed was the mistaken removal of the prized tree. Over 60 years later, despite the error, no street tree appears to have been replanted at this location and the gravel strip is used for parking cars.

Threats abound. Over 100 million ash trees have been lost across 15 states since the first emerald ash borer was sighted in Michigan in 2002, a beetle attracted to the specific odor and color of ash trees. So far, Washington has remained unscathed, but it is only a matter of a time: one was sighted in Oregon in 2022.

Out of Seattle's 4,331 ash right-of-way trees, which are responsible for removing one million pounds of carbon dioxide from our atmosphere each year, District 3, which includes the Central District, has the most. While the current-day Central District spans many neighborhoods, the northern area became known as Cherry Hill because it was home to the Cherry Hill "urban renewal project" (1959 to 1976), which resulted in over 1,000 structures being razed.

Oregon ash (*Fraxinus latifolia*)
925 E. Alder St.

Ash
"the tree of grandeur"
FRAXINUS
DECIDUOUS
Total: 4,331 (2.5% of all right-of-way trees in Seattle)

Green Ash
(FRAXINUS PENNSYLVANICA)
Max Height: 145'

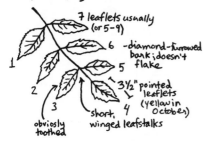

- 7 leaflets usually (or 5-9)
- 6 –diamond-furrowed bark; doesn't flake
- 5
- 3½" pointed leaflets (yellow in October)
- short, winged leafstalks
- obviously toothed

FROM EAST AND CENTRAL N. AMERICA

① Tied as third-widest diameter ash street tree in Seattle: 909 18th Ave.; listed incorrectly in city's data as a "flame" narrow-leafed Caucasian ash

② Tied as fourth-widest diameter ash street tree in Seattle: 1516 E. Pike St.

③ 1416 E. Marion St.; listed incorrectly in city's data as "Oregon ash"

Narrowleaf Ash
(FRAXINUS AUGUSTIFOLIA)
Max Height: 100'

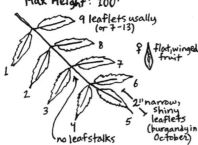

- 9 leaflets usually (or 7-13)
- 8
- ♀ flat, winged fruit
- 7
- 6
- 2" narrow, shiny leaflets (burgandy in October)
- no leafstalks

FROM SW EUROPE, N. AFRICA, W. ASIA

④ 118 22nd Ave., a cultivar patented in 1965 called 'Flame' narrowleaf ash

Oregon Ash
(FRAXINUS LATIFOLIA)
Max Height: 150'
(NATIVE from SW B.C. to S. California)

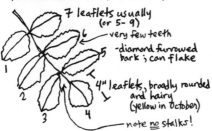

- 7 leaflets usually (or 5-9)
- very few teeth
- –diamond furrowed bark; can flake
- 4" leaflets, broadly rounded and hairy (yellow in October)
- note no stalks!

European Ash
(FRAXINUS EXCELSIOR)
Max Height: 150'
(from Europe, Asia Minor)

- 11 leaflets usually (toothed edges)
- 10
- ♀ flat, winged fruit
- 9
- 8
- black buds on twig tips
- 7
- 3"
- no leafstalk

44

Manna Ash
(FRAXINUS ORNUS)

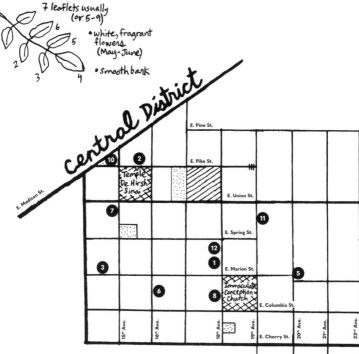

7 leaflets usually (or 5-9)

• white, fragrant flowers (May-June)

• smooth bark

Central District

E. Pine St.

E. Madison St.

E. Pike St.

Temple De Hirsh Sinai

E. Union St.

E. Spring St.

Immaculate Conception Church

E. Marion St.

E. Columbia St.

15th Ave.

16th Ave.

18th Ave.

19th Ave.

20th Ave.

21st Ave.

22nd Ave.

E. Cherry St.

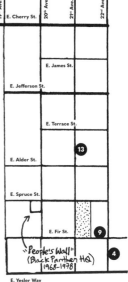

E. James St.

E. Jefferson St.

E. Terrace St.

E. Alder St.

E. Spruce St.

E. Fir St.

"People's Wall" (Black Panther HQ) 1968-1978

E. Yesler Way

Also see:

- **Widest diameter ash street tree when including right-of-way data:** Delridge, European ash (6351 18th Ave. SW)
- **Tied as widest diameter ash street tree in Seattle:** Eastlake, Oregon Ash (85 E. Roanoke St.). *Not illustrated:* East Capitol Hill, green ash (704 Bellevue Ave. E.)
- **Tied as second-widest diameter ash street tree in Seattle:** *Not illustrated:* Phinney Ridge, European ash (603 N. 49th St.) and Delridge, European ash (6745 18th Ave. SW)
- **Third-widest diameter ash street tree in Seattle:** *Not illustrated:* Central District, green ash (925 E. Alder St.)
- **Tied as fourth- and sixth-widest diameter ash street trees in Seattle:** Capitol Hill SE, green ash (131 13th Ave. E.)
- **Tied as sixth-widest ash street trees in city:** Capitol Hill, manna ash (224 14th Ave. E.); *Not illustrated:* narrowleaf ash (600 Broadway E.)

45

Green ash (*Fraxinus pennsylvanica*)
1516 E. Pike. St.
Across the street is Temple De Hirsch Sinai, formed in 1899 with a sanctuary completed in this location in 1908 and the current temple completed in 1960. Jimi Hendrix played his first gig here in the temple's Jaffe Room and, the following year in 1961, Martin Luther King, Jr. was invited to speak when other religious leaders in the city wouldn't host him.

other notable street trees:

Bigleaf Maple
(ACER MACROPHYLLUM)

5 lobes (9" or more)

- **5** Tied for sixth-widest diameter maple street tree in Seattle: 910 20th Ave.

Black Locust
(ROBINIA PSEUDOACACIA)

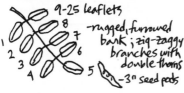

9-25 leaflets

-rugged, furrowed bark; zig-zaggy branches with double thorns

-3" seed pods

- **6** Tied for fifth-widest diameter black locust street tree in Seattle: 828 16th Ave.

English Holly
(ILEX AQUIFOLIUM)

3½

.stiff, glossy, prickly leaves

- **7** Tied as widest diameter English holly street tree in Seattle: 1129 15th Ave., very few prickles

European Beech
(FAGUS SYLVATICA)

3" oval leaf with wavy edge

-smooth gray bark like elephant skin

- **8** Second-widest diameter beech street tree in Seattle: 815 18th Ave.

Lawson Cypress
(CHAMAECYPARIS LAWSONIANA)

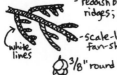

- reddish bark, broad ridges; drooping leader

-scale-like foliage in fan-shaped sprays

white lines

3/8" round seed cone

- **9** Third-widest diameter false cypress street trees in Seattle: 2120 E. Fir St.

London Plane
(PLATANUS ACERIFOLIA)

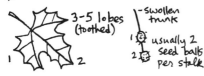

3-5 lobes (toothed)

-swollen trunk

usually 2 seed balls per stalk

10 11th-widest diameter plane street tree in Seattle: 1425 E. Madison St., with others

Northern Catalpa
(CATALPA SPECIOSA)

←long stalk

8" heart-shaped leaf

-contorted branches

14" seed pod

-bell-shaped flowers (late-June/early-July)

11 Widest diameter catalpa street tree in Seattle: 1124 19th Ave.; listed only as "catalpa"

Red Oak
(QUERCUS RUBRA)

- broad, ridged bark

7" shallow-lobed leaf, often with red stem

1" acorn

12 Fourth-widest diameter oak street tree in Seattle: 921 18th Ave.

Japanese Hill Cherry
(PRUNUS JAMASAKURA)
Max height: 82'

• young foliage is reddish-brown; mature leaves green, slender, and whitish on underside
• white flowers (late-March)
• 5 petals in clusters of 2-5
• small cherries (inedible) in June

13 Widest and second-widest diameter cherry street trees in Seattle: 312 and 300 21st Ave., mistakenly listed in city's data as Sargent cherry; according to local tree expert Arthur Lee Jacobson, "Most likely the situation was simply that Japanese Hill Cherry and Sargent Cherry were confused at the nursery" (note single 'Kwanzan' cherry at 308)

COLUMBIA CITY
walnut

California began growing its first walnut orchards by the 1870s, but the Pacific Northwest was slower on the uptake. "The knowledge that nut trees are of slow growth and that trees planted now will not reach their prosperous bearing stage until the appearance of the next generation often deters the planting," the *Seattle Daily Times* reported in a 1903 article. Two decades must have seemed like a long time to wait in a boom-and-bust town like Seattle, so the *Times* added that "it is one of the responsibilities of life to build for the future."

The state horticulturist at the time stated that it was always "assumed that the walnut would not grow in this northern latitude," but he went on to explain that "the farmers who planted the walnut trees and who were disappointed in the failure of the fruit to mature, did not cut out the trees" and that "they are now gratified in observing that the trees they planted fifteen or eighteen years ago have themselves matured and are producing big crops of nuts." Today, the fruits of fewer than 240 walnut trees in the right-of-way remain as evidence of the altruism of past Seattleites.

District 2, where Columbia City is located, has only 23 walnut right-of-way trees, but it is home to both the first recorded and some of the widest in diameter. Once a densely forested independent town bordered by marshlands, Columbia City was home to Hitt Fireworks Company (1905 to 1960s), one of the largest manufacturers of fireworks in the United States in the early 20th century.

Black walnut (*Juglans nigra*)
4803 S. Lucile St.

Walnut
"the tree of intellect"
JUGLANS
DECIDUOUS

Total: 238 (0.1% of all right-of-way trees in Seattle)

Black Walnut
(JUGLANS NIGRA)
Max Height: 165'

13-27 pointed leaflets (toothed)
(pure yellow in fall)

- furrowed bark in diamond-shaped pattern; dark

dull

2" round nut with grooves (in green husk) (edible but beware black stains!)

English Walnut
(JUGLANS REGIA)
Max Height: 120'

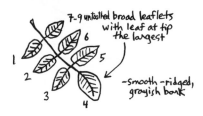

7-9 untoothed broad leaflets with leaf at tip the largest

- smooth-ridged, grayish bark

glossy

2½" nuts with smooth ridges (edible)

Ripe: Mid-September

FROM EASTERN N. AMERICA

1 **Fourth- and sixth-widest walnut street trees in the city: 4803 and 4807 S. Lucile St.**

2 5100 46th Ave. S.: in private yard hanging over sidewalk shaped around it; not included in data even though it is in the right-of-way

3 **First-recorded walnut street tree in Seattle: 5011 S. Brandon St.; listed incorrectly as English walnut on July 24, 1981—about a week before music network MTV would launch**

FROM MIDDLE EAST, BALKANS

4 4917 43rd Ave. S., right-of-way tree hanging over sidewalk

Columbia City

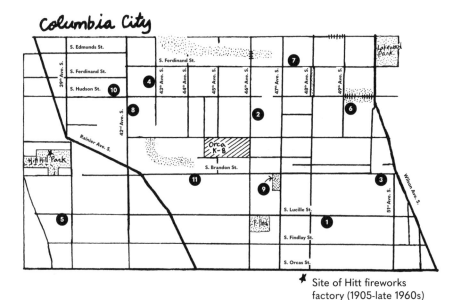

⭑ Site of Hitt fireworks
factory (1905-late 1960s)

Also see:

- **Widest walnut street tree in Seattle:** Greenwood, black walnut (7032 2nd Ave. NW)
- **Second-widest walnut street tree in Seattle:** Queen Anne, black walnut (1620 7th Ave. W.)
- **Fifth-widest walnut street tree in Seattle:** Phinney Ridge, butternut (6048 1st Ave. NW)
- **Seventh-widest walnut street tree in Seattle:** Phinney Ridge, black walnut (203 N. 60th St.)
- **Second-widest English walnut street tree in Seattle:** *Not illustrated:* University District (5706 17th Ave. NE)
- **Third-widest English walnut street tree in Seattle:** Ravenna (6524 16th Ave. NE)
- **Tied for 13th-widest walnut street trees in Seattle:** Wallingford, black walnut (1818 N. 43rd St.) and Madison Valley, English walnut (1607 33rd Ave
- **Third-widest walnut street tree in Seattle:** Capitol Hill, hybrid walnut (1223 18th Ave. E.)
- **Widest English walnut street tree in Greenwood:** (131 N. 81st St.)
- **First-recorded and overall widest walnut when including right-of-way trees:** Leschi, black walnut (800 Hiawatha Pl. S.)

other notable street trees:

Bigleaf Maple
(ACER MACROPHYLLUM)

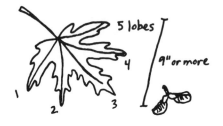

5 lobes
9" or more

5 First-recorded maple street tree in Seattle: 3843 S. Lucile St.; listed on July 24, 1950—the day the first rocket was launched at Cape Canaveral, Florida; astronauts landed on the moon 19 years later

'Akebono' Yoshino Cherry
(PRUNUS X YEDOENSIS 'AKEBONO')

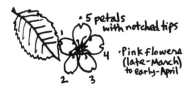

5 petals with notched tips
Pink flowers (late-March) to early-April

6 Widest 'Akebono' cherry street trees in Columbia City: 5040 49th Ave. S., row of street trees

Southern Catalpa
(CATALPA BIGNONIOIDES)

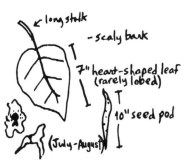

long stalk
scaly bark
7" heart-shaped leaf (rarely lobed)
10" seed pod
(July-August)

7 10th-widest catalpa street tree in Seattle: 4702 S. Ferdinand St.

Common Orchard Apple
(MALUS X DOMESTICA)

3" toothed leaf

-spreading, twisted tree with tangled branches

1 1/4 light pink flowers with 5 petals (March to mid-April)

green to red fruit, 5" or more

8 Tied as second-widest common orchard apple street tree in District 2: 5016 42nd Ave. S., possibly a wild specimen next to yard barrier

9 Dawson St. & 47th Ave. S.: SW corner, many at Brandon Street Orchard (not included in data)

'kwanzan' flowering Cherry
(PRUNUS 'KWANZAN')

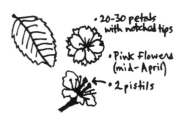

• 20-30 petals with notched tips

• Pink flowers (mid-April)

• 2 pistils

10 Widest Kwanzan cherry street trees in Columbia City: 3952 S. Hudson St., row of street trees

Western Red Cedar
(THUJA PLICATA)

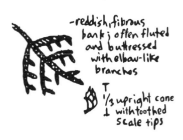

-reddish, fibrous bark; often fluted and buttressed with elbow-like branches

1/3 upright cone with toothed scale tips

11 Second-widest western red cedar street tree in Seattle: 4431 S. Brandon St.

SEWARD PARK
"the Magnificent Forest"
(1911)

Seward Park has the one of nation's largest surviving stands of unlogged old growth forest in a major urban city. On Earth Day in 2022, President Joe Biden visited the park to sign an executive order to inventory old-growth trees.

1 *Atlas cedar (Cedrus atlantica)*
East Shore Loop road, behind a decorative stone bridge near the Fish Hatchery trailhead; the 20 hatchery ponds were begun as a Depression-era Works Progress Administration (WPA) project in 1935 and were decommissioned in 1978

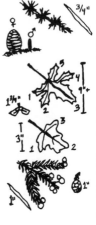

2 *Bigleaf maple (Acer macrophyllum)*
East side of Lost Lake trail, a fallen "fairy tree" with its roots exposed and many younger trees growing out of its trunk

3 *Bolleana poplar (Populus alba 'Pyramidalis')*
A row lining the shore by the south parking lot

4 *Coast redwood (Sequoia sempervirens)*
Near the beach, west of the pottery studio, two trees growing together (a phenomena known as "crown shyness" helps trees avoid growing directly into each other)

5 *Douglas fir (Pseudotsuga menziesii)*
Widest diameter Douglas fir in the city's data (also a Heritage Tree) in northern part of main forest trail; it is topped and has burn marks likely from controlled fires set by the Indigenous people who managed this land to encourage growth

6 *Garry oak (Quercus garryana)*
East of the south parking lot, by the footpath is one of the last remaining natural groves of Seattle's only native oak.

7 *Pacific madrona (Arbutus menziesii)*
North of the boulder on the Erratic trail, a tree right on the footpath with its red trunk leaning west almost horizontally

8 *Western red cedar (Thuja plicata)*
Northwest part of park, an old cedar grove with a fire-hollowed giant and another large one where the trail bends south

9 *Austrian pine (Pinus nigra)*
On the inner loop road near Shelter #5, a specimen with a large branch curling to the ground and back up again

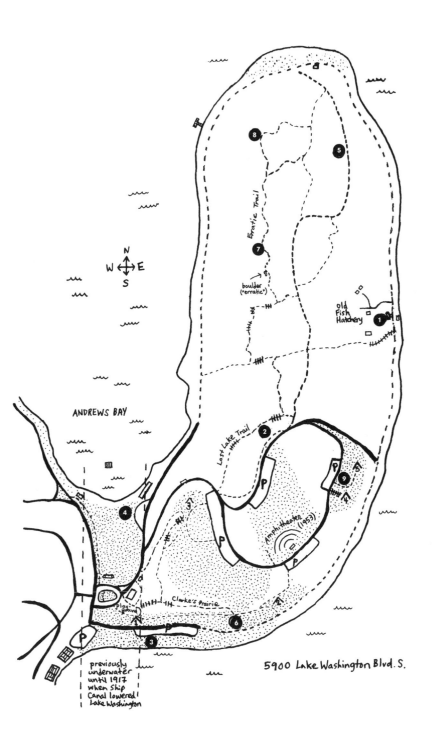

N
W E
S

ANDREWS BAY

Erratic Trail

boulder
("erratic")

Old
Fish
Hatchery

1

8

5

7

Lost Lake Trail

2

9

4

Amphitheater
(1953)

Clarke's Prairie

Play
ground

6

3

previously
underwater
until 1917
when Ship
Canal lowered
Lake Washington

5900 Lake Washington Blvd. S.

DELRIDGE
Madrone

Much of the Pacific madrona's favorite areas to grow along the West Coast, from southern British Columbia to California, have been converted to residential development. As Seattle continues to grow, old madronas have become less common here, as they are extremely dependent on their specific habitats and are notoriously difficult to transplant because of their deep roots and complex fungal relationships.

"People are . . . unanimously puzzled about what might be causing [the tree's] apparent decline in urban areas of the Pacific Northwest," stated a 1995 University of Washington report. Sadly, puzzlement about missing madronas is a longstanding Seattle tradition.

Dubbed "The Battle of the Boulevard," the distinctive madrona trees along Magnolia Boulevard began mysteriously disappearing, cut and removed by supposed vandals beginning in 1930. The following year, the park board noted with horror 41 madrona trees with "rings cut around their trunks." Then, a few years after that in 1935, accusations took a more pointed angle when the board requested "to arrest or fine [any] property owner who illegally cuts a tree on the boulevard." Apparently some homeowners had been discovered secretly felling trees to clear views. Entrenched neighbors drew lines and vigilantes were born, with the madrona feud documented well into the 1950s (and some say even into the present).

Seattle has 600 madrone right-of-way trees, with District 7, where Delridge is located, claiming the most.

Pacific madrona (*Arbutus menziesii*)
6701 13th Ave. SW

Madrone

"the tree of true love"
ARBUTUS
EVERGREEN
Total: 600 (0.3% of all right-of-way trees in Seattle)

Pacific Madrona
(ARBUTUS MENZIESII)
Max Height: 130'

- gnarled, crooked, leaning tree
- reddish bark peeling to reveal smooth green on upper trunk; rough scales at base

4" leathery leaf

⅜" red berries in clusters (October)

⅓"

6" spikes of tiny "urn"-shaped white flowers (March-May)

BC TO S. CALIFORNIA

1. Widest diameter Pacific madrona street tree in Seattle: 6701 13th Ave. SW (on SW Holly St.)

2. Fourth-widest diameter Pacific madrona street tree in Seattle: SW Webster St. and 12th Ave. SW, traffic circle

3. Tied for fifth-widest diameter Pacific madrona street tree in Seattle: 1910 SW Holly St., next to fence

4. Tied for fifth-widest diameter Pacific madrona street tree in Seattle: 8110 7th Ave. SW, next to parking strip

Strawberry Tree
(ARBUTUS UNEDO)
Max Height: 30'
- shrub-like tree
- reddish, shredding bark

2-4" glossy leaf

¾" spiky red fruit (October-December)

- white "urn"-shaped flowers; tiny, in bushels (September-December)

2"

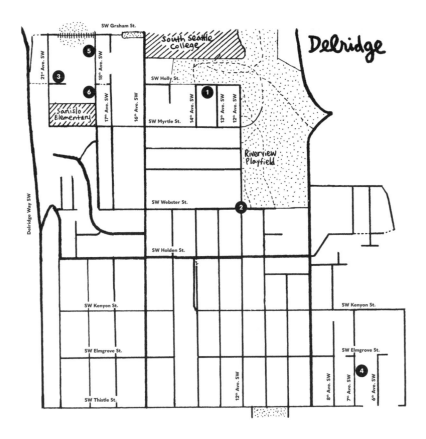

Also see:

- **Second-widest diameter Pacific madrona street tree in Seattle:** Magnolia (3232 29th Ave. W.)
- **Third-widest diameter Pacific madrona street tree in Seattle:** Madison Valley (1618 29th Ave.)
- **Tied for fifth-widest diameter Pacific madrona street tree in Seattle:** Magnolia (2595 Crestmont Pl. W.)
- **Widest diameter strawberry tree street tree in Seattle:** Capitol Hill (1018 E. Thomas St.)

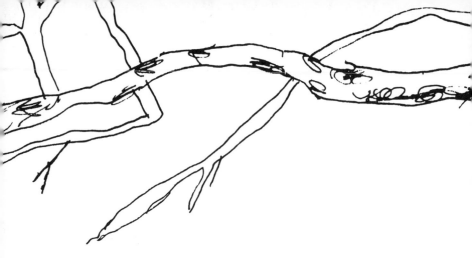

DELRIDGE
OTHER NOTABLE STREET TREES:

European Ash
(FRAXINUS EXCELSIOR)

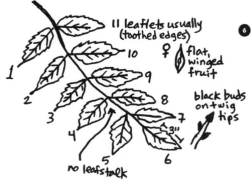

11 leaflets usually
(toothed edges)

♀ flat, winged fruit

black buds on twig tips

3"

no leafstalk

5 Widest diameter ash street tree when including right-of-way data: 6351 18th Ave. SW, next to mailboxes; listed only as "Ash (*Fraxinus sp.*)"

6 Tied as second-widest diameter ash street tree in Seattle when including right-of-way data: 6745 18th Ave. SW, between driveways; listed only as "Ash (*Fraxinus sp.*)"

European ash (*Fraxinus excelsior*)
6351 18th Ave. SW

London plane (*Platanus acerifolia*)
600 1st Ave.

DOWNTOWN
Plane

Known for its ability to withstand pollution, the London plane tree was the most common street tree in the world in the 19th century. In Seattle, many were planted for the 1962 World's Fair, although one of those on Cedar Street was brazenly chopped down in 1970 in broad daylight by the owner of the adjacent 5 Point Cafe.

"The roots got into the city fire-alarm system wiring and I poured creosote all over the roots but it just grew all the faster," he explained shamelessly to reporters. The $150 fine for illegally removing a street tree—established only three years prior—apparently had not deterred the café owner, whose $1,000 sign had been obscured by the tree. "I've blown $150 in a lot worse ways," he was quoted as saying. The city took the merchant activist to court, and the incident prompted the rewriting of Seattle's street tree ordinance, tripling the fine from its previous maximum.

That same decade, the city's arborist complained that plane trees were responsible for "more damage claims for injuries from falls than our nearly 20,000 other trees." Then, in 1984, all hell broke loose when the city attempted to cut down five silver maples in Pioneer Square because they were not officially designated plane trees. The *Seattle Daily Times* called it "a confrontation which nearly ended in a fistfight" between city crews and the concerned citizen who had planted the maples. (The maples lost.)

Downtown has more than half the city's apparently controversial plane street trees, overall responsible for removing one million pounds of carbon dioxide from our atmosphere each year. The last original tree in the downtown area was logged in 1879.

Plane
"the tree of genius"
PLATANUS
DECIDUOUS
Total : 1,891 (1.1% of all right-of-way trees in Seattle)

greenish, gray-brown bark is smooth and mottled with creamish colors

London Plane vs. *American Sycamore*

checkered

American Sycamore
(PLATANUS OCCIDENTALIS)
Max Height : 176'

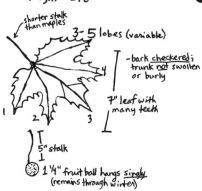

shorter stalk than maples

3-5 lobes (variable)

-bark checkered; trunk not swollen or burly

7" leaf with many teeth

5" stalk

1 ¼" fruit ball hangs singly (remains through winter)

FROM EAST AND SOUTH N. AMERICA

1 220 1st Ave. S., second tree north of Main St. is listed in the city's data as American sycamore; the bark is checkered and scaly, like an American sycamore, and the trunk isn't swollen and burly like a London plane, but this is still probably a London plane (Pioneer Square's "official" tree)

London Plane
(PLATANUS X ACERIFOLIA)
Max Height: 150'

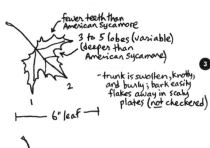

fewer teeth than American sycamore

3 to 5 lobes (variable) (deeper than American Sycamore)

-trunk is swollen, knotty, and burly; bark easily flakes away in scaly plates (not checkered)

6" leaf

seed balls hang usually two per stalk, but can be also one or three+

EUROPEAN HYBRID OF AMERICAN SYCAMORE AND MIDDLE EAST'S ORIENTAL PLANE

2 Occidental Park (200 Occidental Ave. S.): Widest at Occidental Ave. S. & S. Main St. (NE side), planted in 1965 but listed in the city's data in 1990

3 **Widest diameter and only Heritage plane street tree in Pioneer Square: 600 1st Ave.,** north side of street, near the Pioneer Square pergola; it is near here that Seattle's first street trees (maples) were located, in front of Henry and Sarah Yesler's old home

4 2005 5th Ave., lining street below Monorail tracks

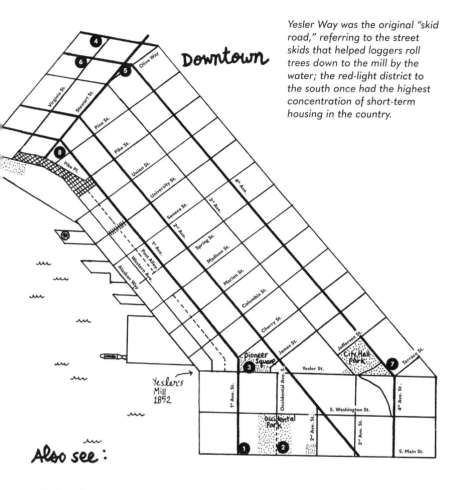

Yesler Way was the original "skid road," referring to the street skids that helped loggers roll trees down to the mill by the water; the red-light district to the south once had the highest concentration of short-term housing in the country.

Also see:

- **Widest diameter plane street tree in Seattle:** University District, London plane (4123 12th Ave. NE)
- **Second- and third-widest diameter plane street tree in Seattle:** Ballard, London planes (2644 NW 60th St.)
- **Fourth-widest diameter plane street tree in Seattle:** SW Capitol Hill, London plane (734 16th Ave. E.)
- **Fifth-widest diameter plane street tree in Seattle:** *Not illustrated:* East Capitol Hill, London plane (Bellevue Pl. E. & Belmont Ave. E., mini park)
- **Widest diameter American sycamore street tree in Seattle (12th-widest plane overall):** Leschi (128 30th Ave.)
- **11th-widest diameter plane street tree in Seattle:** Wallingford, London plane (2219 N. 46th St.)
- **13th-widest diameter plane street tree in Seattle:** Cherry Hill, London plane (15th Ave. & E. Madison St., mini park)
- **Mount Baker's widest diameter street tree:** London plane (3232 37th Pl. S.)

other notable street trees:

Giant Sequoia
(SEQUOIADENDRON GIGANTEAM)

- red, fibrous, ridged bark
- cord-like twigs with tiny sharp scale-like "leaves"

T 2½" cone

5 Downtown's most famous giant sequoia (out of only two total): Triangle at 4th Ave., Stewart St. & Olive Way

A Deeper Dig

The giant sequoia in front of the old Bon Marché, then Macy's, department store was transplanted to the retail core in 1973, when it was about 16 years old. At the time, park planners predicted the tree would "withstand the air pollution caused by traffic because it has grown for years near Aurora Avenue."

In 2010, Seattle's Department of Transportation doubted the tree would survive, given what the *Seattle Times* described as "its current environment of pavement and car exhaust." Then, in 2016, the tree unexpectedly made national news, briefly trending on Twitter (#ManInTree) when a man climbed its branches, remaining there for more than 24 hours, while traffic was stopped and police attempted to coax him down.

Red Oak
(QUERCUS RUBRA)

-broad ridged bark

7" shallow-lobed leaves often with red stems

1" acorns

6 **First-recorded street trees in downtown:** 2001 4th Ave., three trees listed on March 1, 1961—the same day US president John F. Kennedy established the Peace Corps by Executive Order 10924; since the program's inception, 240,000 Americans have served in 142 countries

Sweetgum
(LIQUIDAMBAR STYRACIFLUA)

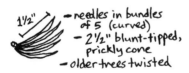

5-7 finely toothed lobes

4 / 5" star-shaped leaf

1" spiky fruit →

Max height: 200'

7 **Widest diameter sweet gum street tree in Downtown:** 410 4th Ave. (illustrated on right)

Bristlecone Pine
(PINUS ARISTATA)

1½"

- needles in bundles of 5 (curved)
- 2½" blunt-tipped, prickly cone
- older trees twisted

8 **Second-widest diameter bristlecone pine street tree in Seattle:** 86 Pine St., tiny and potted; this particular tree makes a cameo in the 1993 movie *Sleepless in Seattle* when Tom Hanks's character walks down Pine Ave. toward Pike Place Market for lunch at the Athenian Inn with his friend (Rob Reiner). Bristlecone pines are the oldest living nonclonal species on the planet with one tree in Eastern California verified to be over 4,800 years old, predating Egypt's pyramids

A Deeper Dig

In 1966, celebrated local architect Victor Steinbrueck expressed "cause for complete concern" over what he derisively called "the situation on Stewart Street."

"The Sweet Gum trees which were planted are much too small and too sparse," he bemoaned. "Unfortunately, the sad results on Stewart Street indicate that no one is responsible there and that the city needs professional guidance in these matters."

EASTLAKE
willows

Willows were planted as street trees in many US cities beginning in the 1830s, until people discovered their twisted and sprawling shapes might not be ideal for curbside placement. By the 1840s, willows were planted almost exclusively in parks adjacent to the water or in cemeteries. Despite these trends, Seattle still planted willow street trees into the early 20th century.

Seattle also lays claim to some willow legend. When Napoléon Bonaparte was exiled to the island of Saint Helena in 1814, he reportedly found solace sitting under the drape of a specific willow tree. Cuttings from that willow were planted at George Washington's grave at Mount Vernon, and American Civil War veteran and attorney general for then Washington Territory J. B. Metcalfe took a cutting from *that* tree in Virginia and planted it at his home in Seattle (located today east of I-5, on property belonging to the Seattle Housing Authority). When I-5 was being developed in the 1960s, citizens asked that the "Napoleon willow" be fenced off and protected, to no avail. Still, the storied tree—a symbol of one man's refuge in a state of exile—lived on into the aughts, visible only from the freeway. The tree is no longer there, but rumor has it that Metcalfe's son planted several cuttings in other Seattle locations, which time may eventually reveal.

There are roughly 358 right-of-way willow trees within city limits. Eastlake is home to both the widest in diameter and the first recorded in Seattle. Once an industrial area bordered by floating shanties, Eastlake was also home to a seaplane hanger located at the foot of Roanoke Street that became the first assembly site for Bill Boeing's earliest plane.

Corkscrew willow (*Salix matsudana 'Tortuosa'*)
2912 Fairview Ave. E.

Willow "the tree of recovery"
SALIX
DECIDUOUS
Total: 358 (0.2% of all right-of-way trees in Seattle)

♂ catkin ♀

- many "burls" and sprout shoots from trunk
- long, flexible twigs

Corkscrew Willow
(Salix matsudana 'Tortuosa')
Max height: 75'

- twisted branches and curly leaves

FROM CHINA, E. SIBERIA, KOREA

① 2912 Fairview Ave. E., at entrance of Fairview Park across water

Golden Weeping Willow
(Salix chrysocoma)

- leafs out late-March
- catkins (April/May)

3-5"

- tip turned to one side
- weeping branches (bright gold)

FROM EUROPE

② **Widest diameter willow tree in Seattle (when including right-of-way trees):** 2321 Fairview Ave. E., bordering parking lot at entrance of Willow Dock Cooperative; listed incorrectly as a Babylon weeping willow

③ 10 Roanoke St., three trees by water at mini park, mistakenly listed as Babylon weeping willows in the city's data

④ **First-recorded weeping willow tree in Seattle (when including right-of-way trees):** 2351 Fairview Ave. E., at entrance of Phoenix Moorage; mistakenly listed as a black willow, on January 1, 1951—the same day a headline in the *Seattle Daily Times* proclaimed: "1950 northwest income soars to new peak" (Beginning in 1980, Washington per capita personal income has been higher than the US average almost every year)

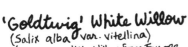

Eastlake

'Goldtwig' White Willow
(Salix alba var. vitellina)
(variant of White Willow from Europe, NW Africa, W. Asia)

2-3"

(whitish underneath)

5 Second-widest diameter willow tree in Seattle (when including right-of-way trees): 2057 Fairview Ave. E., south of Wandesford Dock, a rare female willow hybrid (listed incorrectly as a Babylon weeping willow in the city's data)

• partly weeping (olive/orange twigs)
• catkins (April) + leaves

Also see :

- **City's widest diameter weeping willow street tree in a planting strip:** Leschi, golden weeping willow (528 26th Ave. S.)
- **City's second-widest diameter weeping willow street tree in a planting strip:** Mount Baker, golden weeping willow (4024 37th Ave. S.)

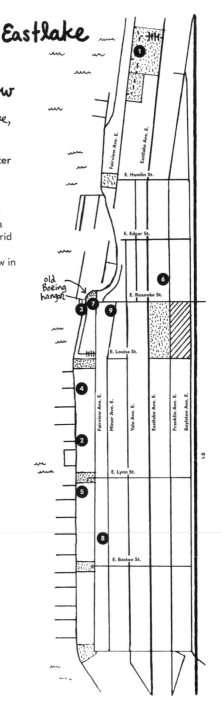

other notable street trees :

Black Locust
(ROBINIA PSEUDOACACIA)

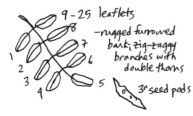

9-25 leaflets

—rugged furrowed bark; zig-zaggy branches with double thorns

3" seed pads

6 Widest diameter black locust street tree in Eastlake: 2611 E. Franklin St.

Lombardy Poplar
(POPULUS NIGRA 'ITALICA')

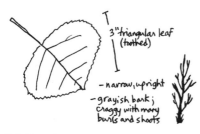

3" triangular leaf (toothed)

— narrow, upright

— grayish bark; craggy with many burls and shoots

7 Third-widest diameter poplar tree in Seattle (when including right-of-way trees): 10 Roanoke St., by the water at Roanoke Street mini park

Silk Tree
(ALBIZIA JULIBRISSIN)

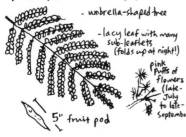

- umbrella-shaped tree

- lacy leaf with many sub-leaflets (folds up at night!)

pink puffs of flowers (late-July to late-September)

5" fruit pod

8 Only silk tree street tree in Eastlake (18th-widest overall in city): 2225 Minor Ave.

Oregon Ash
(FRAXINUS LATIFOLIA)

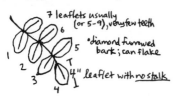

7 leaflets usually (or 5-9), very few teeth

•diamond furrowed bark; can flake

4" leaflet with no stalk

9 Widest diameter ash street tree in Seattle: 85 E. Roanoke St. (on Minor Ave. E.)

Golden weeping willow (*Salix 'Chysocoma'*)
2351 Fairview Ave. E. at entrance of Willow Dock Cooperative

Eastern white pine (*Pinus strobus*)
4518 6th Ave. NW

FREMONT
Pines

Pines help regulate urban stormwater in the winter months, when Seattle gets most of its precipitation and when deciduous trees have already lost their leaves. But in 1977, the city arborist admitted that few coniferous evergreens were used in the street tree program due to their shallow root systems. "We are experimentally trying some Ponderosa pines in the Madrona area," he explained. (That experiment continues today in 2023 on 29th Ave. between E. Cherry and E. Union St.)

Despite not being often used as street trees, the nation's history has been shaped by pines, helping to catalyze the American Revolution. In the late 18th century, the best timber for ship masts was from colonial New Hampshire's eastern white pines. The king of England declared that all pines with a diameter greater than 12 inches would automatically become his country's property. This understandably infuriated settlers and ignited what became known as the Pine Tree Riot of 1772, which may have later inspired the Boston Tea Party.

Pines were a hot commodity on the West Coast, too, making up almost 50 percent of western inland forests, but beginning in 1880, they became the principal target of logging. Combined with blister rust, 90 percent of western white pines in the inland Northwest were removed in less than 70 years. Unfortunately for the pine, in the succession of trees, they are typically replaced by other trees like fir.

There are 1,908 pine right-of-way trees in the city, and District 6—which includes most of Fremont—has one of the widest pine street trees in Seattle.

Pine "the tree of courage"

PINUS
EVERGREEN
Total: 1,908 (1.1% of all right-of-way trees in Seattle)

Austrian Black Pine
(PINUS NIGRA)
Max Height: 150'

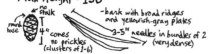

- round base
- no stalk
- bark with broad ridges and yellowish-gray plates
- 4" cones, no prickles (clusters of 1-6)
- 3-5" needles in bundles of 2 (very dense)

FROM CENTRAL AND SOUTH EUROPE

1 4511 Greenwood Ave. N. (with a Japanese black pine north of it)

Eastern White Pine
(PINUS STROBUS)
Max Height: 270'

- long stalk
- purplish-gray, furrowed bark
- no prickles
- 4-8" cones; narrow and hanging in clusters
- 3-5" needles in bundles of 5

FROM CENTRAL AND EAST N. AMERICA

2 Second-widest diameter pine street tree in Seattle: 4518 6th Ave. NW

Lodgepole Pine
(PINUS CONTORTA)
Max Height: 200'

- 4" curved, thin needles in bundles of 2
- 2" oval cone, slightly prickly

NATIVE FROM WESTERN N. AMERICA

3 111 NW 40th St.

Scots Pine
(PINUS SYLVESTRIS)
Max Height: 157'

- scaly bark with upper trunk orange and smooth
- 1-4" stiff, twisted needles in bundles of 2
- blunt tips
- no prickles
- 3" cones

FROM PACIFIC TO ATLANTIC OCEAN TEMPERATE ZONES

4 643 NW 48th St.

Italian Stone Pine
(PINUS PINEA)
Max Height: 120'

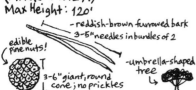

- reddish-brown furrowed bark
- 3-5" needles in bundles of 2
- edible pine nuts!
- 3-6" giant, round cone; no prickles
- umbrella-shaped tree

FROM THE MEDITERRANEAN

5 Third-widest Italian stone pine street tree in Seattle (out of only eight total): 133 NW 44th St.; listed incorrectly as eastern white pine

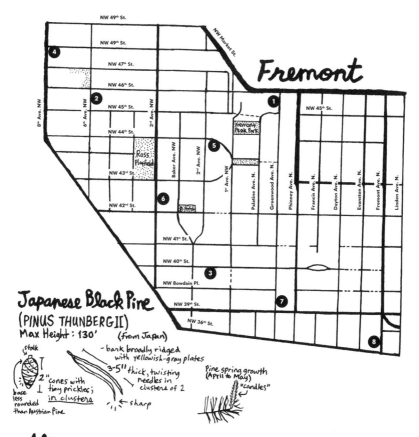

Also see:

- **Widest diameter pine street tree in Seattle:** Wedgwood, eastern white pine (3054 NE 88th St.)
- **Third-widest pine street tree in Seattle:** *Not illustrated:* Madrona, western white pine (910 27th Ave.)
- **Fourth-widest diameter pine street tree in Seattle:** Greenwood, eastern white pine (7034 3rd Ave. NW)
- **Widest diameter Austrian pine street tree in Seattle:** University District (4715 16th Ave. NE)
- **Widest diameter bristlecone pine street tree in Seattle:** Greenwood (640 NW 74th St.)
- **Second-widest diameter bristlecone pine street tree in Seattle:** Downtown (86 Pine St.)
- **Highest concentration of Ponderosa pine street trees in Seattle:** Madrona (widest diameter at 1118 29th Ave.)

FREMONT
other notable street trees :

chinese Windmill Palm
(TRACHYCARPUS FORTUNEI)

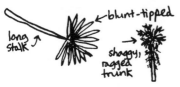

long stalk →

← blunt-tipped

→

shaggy, ragged trunk

6 **Highest concentration of palm street trees in Seattle:** Lining the block, with widest diameter at 4216 3rd Ave. NW

A Deeper Dig

Palms were first popularly used as street trees in the 1930s in Los Angeles to beautify the city for an upcoming Olympic Games, but the palms in Seattle are an entirely different species, native to a region in China that gets colder than the Pacific Northwest. District 6, where most of Fremont is located, has more than half the right-of-way palms in the city, largely due to one citizen, a Fremont resident named Alain Lucier. Beginning in the late 1990s, Lucier single-handedly planted palm street trees on his block at his own cost and, according to a story in the *Seattle Times*, "he remembered some neighbors, who initially had turned down the palms, changing their minds after seeing how they looked."

Also see :

- **First-recorded *and* widest diameter palm street trees in Seattle:** *Not illustrated:* Magnolia; listed August 15, 1986 (2401 W. Armour St.)
- **Only palm street tree in District 2 that is listed in the city's data as an "unknown" species:** Beacon Hill (3117 22nd Ave.)

Black Locust
(ROBINIA PSEUDOACACIA)

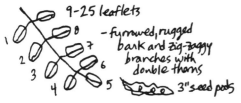

9-25 leaflets

- furrowed, rugged bark and zig-zaggy branches with double thorns

3" seed pods

7 Tied as second-widest diameter black locust street tree: 302 N. 39th St. (on Greenwood Ave. N.)

Bolleana White Poplar
(POPULUS ALBA 'PYRAMIDALIS')
Max Height: 125'

3" leaf (3-5 lobes) with wavy edges

- underleaf is whitish and fuzzy
- whitish bark with black furrows

8 Tied for widest diameter poplar street trees in Seattle: 3635 Fremont Ave. N.; listed only as "white poplar"

Chinese windmill palm (*Trachycarpus fortunei*)
4216 3rd Ave. NW

PINES

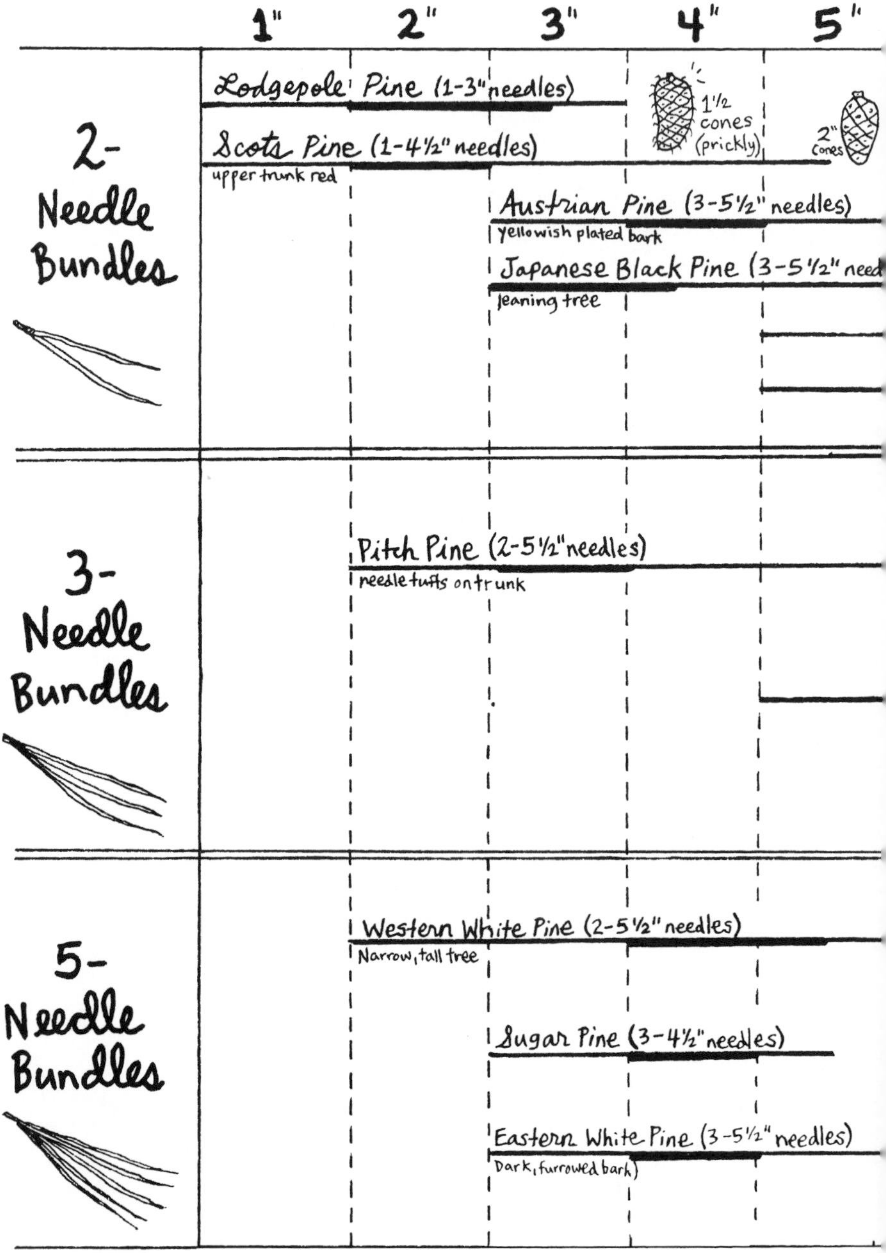

	1"	2"	3"	4"	5"

2- Needle Bundles

Lodgepole Pine (1-3" needles)

Scots Pine (1-4½" needles)
upper trunk red

1½ cones (prickly)

2" cones

Austrian Pine (3-5½" needles)
yellowish plated bark

Japanese Black Pine (3-5½" needles)
leaning tree

3- Needle Bundles

Pitch Pine (2-5½" needles)
needle tufts on trunk

5- Needle Bundles

Western White Pine (2-5½" needles)
Narrow, tall tree

Sugar Pine (3-4½" needles)

Eastern White Pine (3-5½" needles)
Dark, furrowed bark

84

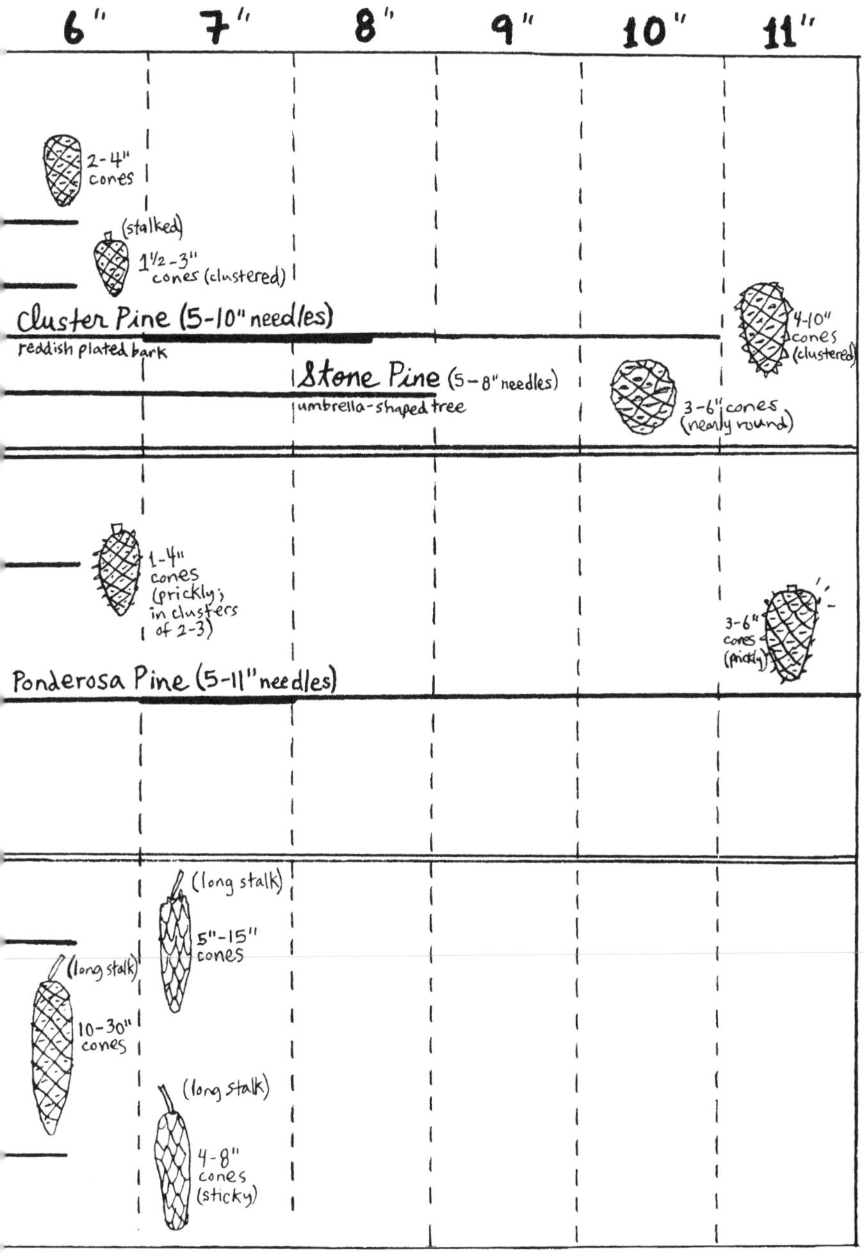

6"	7"	8"	9"	10"	11"

2-4" cones

(stalked)

1½-3" cones (clustered)

Cluster Pine (5-10" needles)
reddish plated bark

Stone Pine (5-8" needles)
umbrella-shaped tree

4-10" cones (clustered)

3-6" cones (nearly round)

1-4" cones (prickly; in clusters of 2-3)

3-6" cones (prickly)

Ponderosa Pine (5-11" needles)

(long stalk)

5"-15" cones

(long stalk)

10-30" cones

(long stalk)

4-8" cones (sticky)

GEORGETOWN
Locusts

The first permanent English settlement in colonial America was built in 1607 from rot-resistant black locust wood, fledgling America's secret weapon. The final British invasion of the northern United States ended in 1814 in the Battle of Lake Champlain because US ships were built with superior locust nails, which held their ships together when they were hit with cannonballs. Meanwhile, the British navy's ships, built with average oak nails, fell apart upon impact. By 1820, the Philadelphia market alone estimated it was exporting up to 100,000 locust nails to England each year.

Black locust also had a brief spell in the early 19th century as a popular fast-growing street tree on the East Coast, but it fell out of favor due to its thorns and pests. California gold miners then brought the tree to the West Coast to grow and use for tunnel timbers, but the tree had a mind of its own. "If you simply cut them they're going to resprout, and then they're going to spread," warned one Pacific Northwest horticulturist. Others concurred, adding they had "seen entire neighborhoods be taken over by these trees." Once a valuable weapon to defeat the British, black locust has beat us now too.

Census Tract 109, which includes King County's oldest neighborhood, Georgetown (annexed by Seattle in 1910), has the lowest percentage of tree canopy cover in the city, but is still home to some of the widest diameter black locust street trees.

Black locust (*Robinia pseudoacacia*)
308 S. Orcas St.

"the tree of friendship"

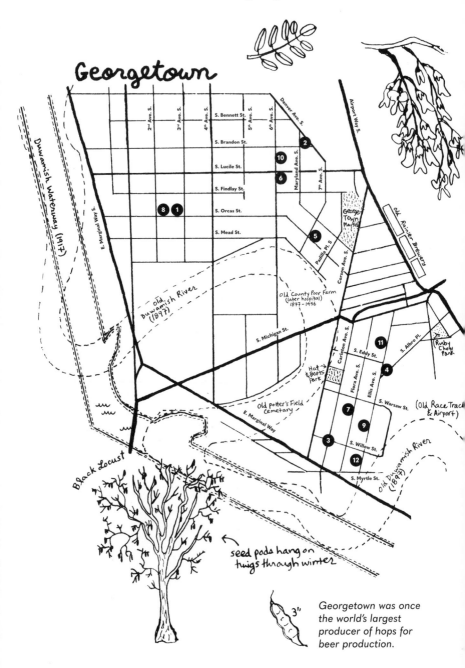

Georgetown

Georgetown was once the world's largest producer of hops for beer production.

seed pods hang on twigs through winter

Black Locust

ROBINIA
DECIDUOUS
Total: 847 (0.5% of all right-of-way trees in Seattle)

Black Locust
(ROBINIA PSEUDOACACIA)
Max Height: 162'

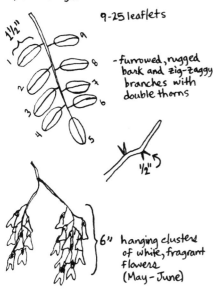

9-25 leaflets

- furrowed, rugged bark and zig-zaggy branches with double thorns

1½"

½"

6" hanging clusters of white, fragrant flowers (May – June)

FROM CENTRAL AND EASTERN UNITED STATES

1 Tied as Seattle's third-widest diameter black locust street tree: 226 S. Orcas St., with others east of 3rd Ave. S.

2 5327 Denver Ave. S., three

3 Carleton Ave. S. & S. Willow St.: in traffic circle, a cultivar called 'Frisia'

4 Ellis Ave. S. & S. Eddy St.: traffic triangle

5 706 S. Orcas St.

Also see:

- **Widest diameter black locust street tree in Seattle:** *Not illustrated:* Magnolia (2600 34th Ave. W.)
- **Tied for second-widest diameter black locust street tree in Seattle:** Fremont (302 N. 39th St.); N. Wedgwood (3022 NE 87th St.)
- **Tied for third-widest diameter black locust street tree in Seattle:** Madrona (1133 35th Ave.); Maple Leaf/Ravenna (7742 16th Ave. NE); West Seattle (5945 48th Ave. SW)
- **Tied for fourth-widest diameter black locust street tree in Seattle:** Loyal Heights (7733 16th Ave. NW)
- **Tied for fifth-widest diameter black locust street tree in Seattle:** Cherry Hill (828 16th Ave.); Greenwood (636 NW 76th St.)
- **Tied for sixth-widest diameter black locust street tree in Seattle:** *Not illustrated:* Fremont (3643 Greenwood Ave. N.); University District/Ravenna (5813 17th Ave. NE)

GEORGETOWN
other notable street trees:

Bigleaf Maple
(ACER MACROPHYLLUM)

6 Second-widest diameter maple street tree in Seattle: a bigleaf maple in Georgetown (5506 6th Ave. S., illustrated on page 22)

Chinese Pistachio
(PISTACIA CHINENSIS)

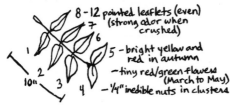

8 - 12 pointed leaflets (even) (strong odor when crushed)

- bright yellow and red in autumn

- tiny red/green flowers (March to May)

- ¼" inedible nuts in clusters

10"

7 Widest diameter pistachio street tree in Seattle (out of only **77** total): 6625 Flora Ave. S.

Evergreen (Southern) Magnolia
(MAGNOLIA GRANDI

6-11" glossy, leathery leaf with brown fuzz underneath

- white flowers late-May

8 Tied as widest diameter, third- and sixth-widest diameter magnolia street trees in Seattle: 222 S. Orcas St., west of black locust

Crape Myrtle
(LAGERSTROEMIA INDICA)

- cinnamon bark peeling to reveal smooth green

2½" leaf with very short leafstalk

- yellow to red in autumn

clusters of fruit capsules remain through winter

- pink flowers at twig tips (September to October)

9 Widest diameter crape myrtle street tree in Seattle: 6653 Ellis Ave. S., with many others on this block, including one intertwined with a rogue apple tree

Lombardy Poplar
(POPULUS NIGRA 'ITALICA')

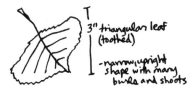

3" triangular leaf (toothed)

-narrow, upright shape with many burls and shoots

10 Widest diameter poplar street trees in Seattle (also the widest street tree in District 2): 601 S. Brandon St. (on 6th Ave. S.)

Loquat
(ERIOBOTRYA JAPONICA)

7" or more glossy, leathery, wrinkled leaf with brown fuzz underneath.

- fruit late spring to early summer
- white flowers (August to January)

11 Tied as second- and fourth-widest diameter loquat street trees in Seattle (out of 13 total): 6285 Ellis Ave. S.

Goldenchain
(LABURNUM X WATERERI)

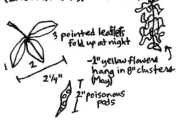

3 pointed leaflets fold up at night

-1" yellow flowers hang in 8" clusters (May)

2¼"

2" poisonous pods

12 Widest diameter goldenchain street tree in Seattle: 6915 Ellis Ave. S., with others on this street

A Deeper Dig

In 1960, a two-year-old girl was treated at Seattle's Children's Orthopedic Hospital after eating a few goldenchain seed pods. By 1963, the hospital reported the trees being the number one culprit of poisoned children in the city, recording 41 related emergency calls. Originally native to the mountains of southern Europe, goldenchain does its best in moderate climates just like the Pacific Northwest's, but perhaps thanks to the scares in the 1960s, there are only roughly 338 goldenchain street trees.

Ginkgo (*Ginkgo biloba*)
5813 McKinley Pl. N.

GREEN LAKE
Ginkgo

After the atomic bomb was dropped on Hiroshima in 1945, six leafing ginkgo trees were the first signs of returning life, providing hope in the wake of horror. Ginkgoes are no strangers to extinction-level events. Once ubiquitous before they were driven off the North American continent by the Ice Age, they are one of the oldest living tree species on the planet and the only tree that scientists believe look identical to how they appeared more than 250 million years ago. But today, they have made their comeback, returning as one of the most planted street trees of our times.

"You see [the ginkgo] all over Tokyo, you see it all over Seoul. But you also see it all over Manhattan," said the dean of the Yale School of Forestry and Environmental Studies in a 2013 interview. "Once you start to recognize ginkgo trees in the urban landscape, you start to see them everywhere."

In 1960, a gardening columnist for the *Seattle Daily Times* wrote that the ginkgo tree "should be used more often for a street tree." Almost a half century later, another columnist in the *Seattle P-I* reported hopefully, "More ginkgoes are appearing on the street!" Today, there are surprisingly still only 1,268 ginkgo street trees in the city, and most have trunks only four inches in diameter or less. To avoid the odor of the tree's fruit, only males are now planted.

Green Lake, named after the green-algae-laden postglacial lake that was lowered in 1911, is part of District 6 and home to the second-widest diameter ginkgo street tree in Seattle as well as a rare female ginkgo.

Ginkgo "the tree of survival"

DECIDUOUS
Total: 1,268 (0.7% of all right-of-way trees in Seattle)

Green Lake

N. 77th St.
N. 75th St.
NE 73rd St.
NE 72nd St.
NE 71st St.
NE 70th St.
NE 68th St.
NE 65th St.
NE 64th St.
NE 63rd St.
NE 62nd St.
NE 61st St.
NE 60th St.
NE 59th St.
NE 58th St.
NE 57th St.
NE 56th St.
NE 55th St.
NE 54th St.
NE 53rd St.

N. 77th St.
Orin Ct. N.
Meridian Ave. N.
Bagley Ave. N.
Corliss Ave. N.
Woodlawn Ave. NE
E. Green Lake Dr. N.
2nd Ave. NE
Latona Ave. NE
6th Ave. NE
NE Maple Leaf Pl.

E. Green Lake Dr. N.
Woodlawn Ave. N
Sunnyside Ave. N.
1st Ave. NE

Green Lake Elementary

John Marshall High

Woodlawn Ave. N
McKinley Pl. N.
Keystone Pl. N.
Kenwood Pl. N.
Meridian Ave. N.
Corliss Ave. N.
1st Ave. NE
Latona Ave. NE
5th Ave. NE

__ School

94

Ginkgo
(GINKGO BILOBA)
Max Height : 200'

FROM E. CHINA

1 **Second-widest diameter ginkgo street tree in Seattle:** 5813 McKinley Pl. N., a male and female (male is wider)

2 7420 Woodlawn Ave. NE

3 6298 Meridian Ave. N., center island, tiny baby male tree planted in 2015

3" fan-shaped leaf (bright yellow October to November)

variable shapes

lopsided, irregular shaped tree with furrowed bark and thick, knobby twigs

flowers like catkins, in clusters (May)

long stalk → ♀ ♂

1" orange fruit; smelly (late September to October)

Also see:

- **Widest diameter ginkgo street tree in the city:** Beacon Hill (1756 S. Spokane St.)
- **First-recorded gingko tree in city data (when including right-of-way trees):** South Park (1032 S. Cloverdale St.)
- **Third-widest diameter ginkgo street tree in Seattle:** Queen Anne (2558 9th Ave. W.)

other notable street trees:

Almond
(PRUNUS DULCIS)

3" shiny, narrow leaf
(toothed)

white or pink
flowers; fragrant
(March)

④ Fourth-widest diameter almond street tree in Seattle: 7700 Meridian Ave. N., on 77th St.

Bigleaf Maple
(ACER MACROPHYLLUM)

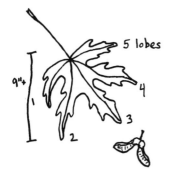

5 lobes

9"+

⑤ Tied for sixth-widest diameter maple street tree in Seattle: 2304 N. 55th St.

Southern Catalpa
(CATALPA BIGNONIOIDES)

long stalk   —scaly bark

7" heart-shaped leaf
2" bell-shaped flower

10" seed pod

⑥ Eighth-widest diameter catalpa street tree in Seattle: 6540 1st Ave. NE; listed only as "catalpa"

Cider Gum Eucalyptus
(EUCALYPTUS GUNNII)

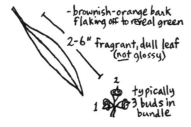

- brownish-orange bark flaking off to reveal green
- 2-6" fragrant, dull leaf (not glossy)
- typically 3 buds in bundle

7 11th-widest diameter eucalyptus street tree in Seattle: 5642 Keystone Pl. N., mystery eucalyptus that looks like a cider gum subspecies with seed capsules in clusters of seven instead of three

Ovens Wattle
(ACACIA PRAVISSIMA)
Max Height: 30'

- small, bushy, weeping tree with whip-like branches
- 1/2" triangular, dull sage-colored leaves
- yellow flowers in ball-like clusters on spikes (February to March)
- 3-4" seed pods

8 Seattle's only acacia street tree: 331 NE 54th St.; listed on Y2K, January 1, 2000

Quince
(CYDONIA OBLONGA)
Max Height: 25'

- 2-4" oval leaf, broad and pointed (toothed)
- Yellow, fuzzy fruit (August to September)
- 2" pale pink flowers with "cupped" petals (April-May)

9 First-recorded quince street trees in Seattle: 107 NE 60th St., a pair; early European settlers in the United States grew quince for its pectin, which was essential for making preserves, but in the 1890s, powdered gelatin made them "obsolete." There are only 19 quince right-of-way trees in the city.

Sitka Spruce
(PICEA SITCHENSIS)
Max height: 317'

- broad crown, scaly bark
- 7/8" prickly, 4-angled needles with white bands underneath
- 2-4" cone with toothed or pointed scales

10 Widest diameter Sitka spruce street tree in Seattle: 321 NE 57th St.

GREENWOOD
Dogwood

In 1916, Seattle's Municipal League announced it was working with the city council on the first plans for a "systematic scheme of planting in the parking strips." J. E. Gould, chair of the organization's city development committee, predicted, "If a mile of [dogwood] trees were successfully grown on both sides of an avenue, they would form, when in full bloom, one of the most beautiful sights that could be enjoyed in any city."

Three years later, in a lecture given to the Sunset Club, University of Washington professor George Burton Riggs singled out the dogwood again: "The dogwood tree would be ideal for a street tree for it is beautiful; blooms twice a year; is of slow growth, doing away with the necessity of entanglement of the branches with the telephone wires, and the taking up of street walks, because of the rapid growth of roots of trees, which is true of those shading the city at present." Dreams do come true: Today, Seattle has over 6,000 dogwood street trees, and they are the sixth-most abundant street tree in the city.

District 6, which includes Greenwood, has the most dogwood street trees in Seattle. Originally a bog known as Woodland, the main road was made of planks to help people maneuver the marshy ground. Trees are known to be some of the best solutions to stormwater runoff, but many neighborhood residents awaited proper drainage into the 1970s.

Pacific dogwood (*Cornus nuttallii*)
644 NW 74th St.

Dogwood "the tree of durability"

CORNUS
DECIDUOUS
Total: 6,222 (3.6% of all right-of-way trees in Seattle)

Eastern Dogwood
(CORNUS FLORIDA)
Max Height: 55'

- twigs curve up at tips; bark cracked and checkered

4½" with veins curving parallel to edge

4 white (or pink) bracts with notched tips (late April to mid-May)

FROM EASTERN N. AMERICA

❶ 621 NW 77th St.; listed as "pink dogwood" in the city's data

❷ 622 NW 81st St., two

Pacific Dogwood
(CORNUS NUTTALLII)
Max Height: 100'

5½" leaf with veins curving parallel to edge

6 white bracts with blunt tips (mid-April to mid-May with a 2nd bloom late August to early October)

NATIVE FROM BC TO CALIFORNIA

❸ **Widest diameter dogwood street tree in Seattle:** 644 NW 74th St.; listed incorrectly in city's data as a hybrid called "Eddie's White Wonder"

Kousa Dogwood
(CORNUS KOUSA)
Max Height: 40'

- thin bark with brown and gray splotches

4" pointed leaf with veins curving parallel to edge

4 white, pointed bracts (June to July)

1" dull red fruit, upright (October)

FROM CHINA, KOREA, JAPAN

❹ 142 NW 75th St., all listed incorrectly in the city's data as "pink dogwood"

❺ 622 NW 78th St., five

❻ 809 NW 77th St., two

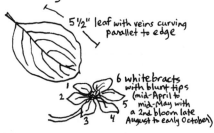

Greenwood

NW 82nd St.

(14) (2) (15) NW 81st St. (11)

Greenwood Elementary (12)
NW 80th St.

NW 79th St. (13)

(5) NW 78th St.

NW 77th St.

(6)

(1)
(7) NW 76th St.

NW 75th St.

(4)

(3) (9) NW 74th St.

NW 73rd St.

NW 72nd St.
(10) (8)

NW 70th St.

5th Ave. NE
3rd Ave. NE
Dibble Ave. NW
8th Ave. NW
6th Ave. NW
2nd Ave. NW
Sycamore Ave. NW
1st Ave. NW
Palatine Ave. N.
Greenwood Ave. N.

Also see:

- **Second-widest diameter dogwood street tree in Seattle:** University District, Pacific dogwood (5225 16th Ave. NE)
- **First-recorded dogwood street trees in Seattle:** Maple Leaf, pink eastern dogwood (8513 4th Ave. N.)

GREENWOOD
other notable street trees:

Black Locust
(ROBINIA PSEUDOACACIA)

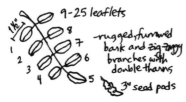

9-25 leaflets
1½"
8 7 6 5
1 2 3 4
—rugged, furrowed bark and zig-zaggy branches with double thorns
3" seed pods

7 Tied for fifth-widest black locust street tree in Seattle: 636 NW 76th St., two

Black Walnut
(JUGLANS NIGRA)

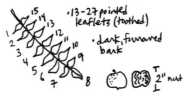

15 14 13 12 11 10 9 8
1 2 3 4 5 6 7
• 13-27 pointed leaflets (toothed)
• dark, furrowed bark
2" nut

8 Widest diameter walnut street tree in Seattle: 7032 NW 72nd St.

Bristlecone Pine
(PINUS ARISTATA)

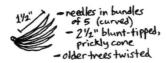

1½"
— needles in bundles of 5 (curved)
— 2½" blunt-tipped, prickly cone
— older trees twisted

9 Widest diameter bristlecone pine street tree in Seattle (out of only two): 640 NW 74th St., tiny tree east of Pacific dogwood; tree rings of the oldest bristlecone pines provide the longest continual climate chronologies on Earth

Eastern White Pine
(PINUS STROBUS)

—furrowed gray bark
3-5" needles (bundles of 5)
4-8" narrow cone with long stem

10 Fourth-widest diameter pine street tree in Seattle: 7034 3rd Ave. NW, with three other eastern white pines on NW 72nd St.

English Walnut
(JUGLANS REGIA)

7-9 broad leaflets
with leaf at tip
the largest

— smooth-ridged
grayish bark

glossy nuts
(mid-September)

11 Widest diameter English walnut street tree in Greenwood: 134 N. 81st St.

Red Oak
(QUERCUS RUBRA)

— broad ridged bark

7" shallow-lobed leaves,
often with red stems

1" acorns

12 Tied as fifth-widest diameter oak street tree in Seattle (also widest overall street tree in Greenwood): 150 NW 80th St., on 1st Ave. NW, with other smaller red oak street trees lining Greenwood Elementary School

Silk Tree
(ALBIZIA JULIBRISSIN)

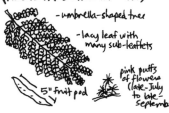

— umbrella-shaped tree

— lacy leaf with
many sub-leaflets

pink puffs
of flowers
(late-July
to late-
September)

5" fruit pod

13 Second-widest diameter silk street tree in Seattle: 332 NW 79th St.

Western Red Cedar
(THUJA PLICATA)

reddish, fibrous bark,
often fluted and
buttressed

— lacy scale-like foliage

1/3" upright cone

14 Second-widest diameter street tree in Greenwood: 650 NW 81st St.

English Holly
(ILEX AQUIFOLIUM)

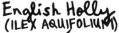
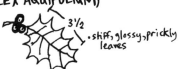

3½

• stiff, glossy, prickly
leaves

15 Third-widest diameter holly street tree in city: 8103 6th Ave. NW, on NW 84th St.

LESCHI
Apples & Crabapples

Washington produces more than 60 percent of the apples grown in the entire United States. There are over 3,000 varieties, but Seattle is one of the only urban environments in the country that still has old orchards with heirloom varieties first planted by early European settlers.

Bavaria-born Andrew and Wilhelmina Piper's orchard in present-day Carkeek Park is one of those heirloom orchards, planted after the Great Seattle Fire of 1889 destroyed their sweet shop in Pioneer Square, forcing them to relocate the family.

Farther south, in the Seward Park neighborhood, at present-day Martha Washington Park, another heirloom orchard was first planted by settler David Graham before a school for "delinquent girls" was opened there in 1920 and the students were forced to tend it.

By the mid-20th century, apple varieties became standardized for commercial production, and many of the individual types of apples grown long ago in Seattle disappeared.

The genus Malus, *including apples and crabapples, is the city's third-most abundant type of street tree, overall responsible for removing one million pounds of carbon dioxide from our atmosphere each year. District 3, which includes Leschi, has the second-most* Malus *street trees in the city as well as the densest concentration of snowdrift and wintergold crabapples. Current-day Leschi Park, once a Nisqually fishing site on Lake Washington, was turned into an amusement park in the late 19th century until it was bought by the City of Seattle and adapted as a public park in the early 20th century.*

Dolgo crabapple (*Malus* 'Dolgo')
937 Davis Pl. S.

Apple & Crabapple

"the tree of transformation"
MALUS
DECIDUOUS
Total: 8,718

(5% of all right-of-way trees in Seattle)

'Dolgo' Crabapple
(MALUS 'DOLGO')
Max Height: 30'

5 petals — earliest to bloom
1 3/4" fragrant, white flowers (mid-April to May)

Common apple leaf rounder, more crumpled

oval with calyx

1 1/2 red, edible fruit (July–August)

FROM RUSSIA

1 City's greatest concentration of 'Dolgo' crabapple street trees: Davis Pl. S., between S. Charles St. and S. Bush Pl.: lining both sides, with widest at 926 Davis Pl. S. (a common orchard apple street tree is just north of it)

Leschi

S. Jackson St.
S. King St.
S. Jackson St.
Frink Park
Washington Middle School
18th Ave. S.
20th Ave. S.
23rd Ave. S.
24th Ave. S.
25th Ave. S.
26th Ave. S.
Martin Luther King Jr. Way S.
S. Lane St.
S. Dearborn St.
Rainier Ave. S.
Hiawatha Pl. S.
Davis Pl. S.
Judkins Park
S. Charles St.
28th Ave. S.
29th Ave. S.
Yakima Ave. S.
30th Ave. S.
31st Ave. S.
32nd Ave. S.
33rd Ave. S.
Yakima Pl. S.
S. Norman St.
S. Judkins St.

- **Widest diameter common orchard apple street tree in Seattle:** *Not illustrated*: North Queen Anne (500 W. Emerson St., in median between W. Bertona St.)
- **Second-widest diameter common orchard apple street tree in Seattle:** Ravenna (7534 21st Ave. NE)
- **Second-widest diameter common orchard apple street tree in District 2:** Columbia City (5016 42nd Ave. S.); widest on Beacon Hill (2508 19th Ave. S.)

Largeleaf Crabapple
(MALUS TSCHONOSKII)
Max Height: 40'

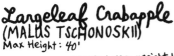

-narrow, very upright tree

Up to 6", thick and leathery; fuzzy beneath (orange to reddish in fall)

1¼ white blossoms; very few (mid-April to May)

1¼" yellowish fruit with reddish cheek; sparse

FROM JAPAN

2 Widest *Malus* street tree in District 3: 2817 S. Lane St., a Japanese cultivar known as being one of the largest kinds of crabapple trees

Profusion Crabapple
(MALUS X MOERLANDII 'PROFUSION')
Max Height: 20'

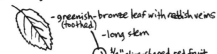

-greenish-bronze leaf with reddish veins (toothed)

-long stem

½" olive-shaped red fruit

1½" deep magenta flowers (late April-early May)

DEVELOPED IN THE NETHERLANDS

3 415 29th Ave. S., with others on 29th Ave. S. from S. Dearborn St. to E. Yesler Way, and on 30th Ave. S. from E. Yesler Way to E. Cherry St.; known for profuse flowers, all but three of the 153 Profusion crabapple street trees in Seattle are concentrated here in Leschi

Snowdrift Crabapple
(MALUS 'SNOWDRIFT')
Max Height: 20'

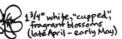

-rounded crown; symmetrical tree; dense branches

-long stem

3/8" orange fruit

glossy leaf with sharp teeth

1¾" white, "cupped", fragrant blossoms (late April - early May)

DEVELOPED IN OHIO IN 1965

4 Greatest concentration of snowdrift crabapple street trees in Seattle: Yakima Pl. S., south of S. Charles St. lining both sides with widest on east side at 904 Yakima Pl. S.; also along Charles St. and Norman St. from MLK Way to 30th Ave. S.

Wintergold Crabapple
(MALUS 'WINTERGOLD')
Max Height: 20'

dark green leaves; yellow in fall

1½" white blossoms; fragrant (relatively late in April)

½" yellow fruit with calyx

calyx →

FROM THE NETHERLANDS

5 Widest diameter wintergold crabapple street tree in Seattle: 539 28th Ave. S. (a common apple mid-block north of it); others line 28th Ave. S. from S. Dearborn St. to S. Jackson St.; all of the city's 107 wintergold crabapple street trees are in Leschi, except two in Ballard

other notable street trees:

Golden Weeping Willow
(SALIX 'CHRYSOCOMA')

- bright gold, flexible twigs
3-5" leaf (toothed)
weeping branches

6 Seattle's widest diameter willow street tree in a planting strip: 528 26th Ave. S., twisted specimen with large hollow and burn marks; listed in city's data incorrectly as Babylon weeping willow (visit soon before it's removed!)

Black Walnut
(JUGLANS NIGRA)

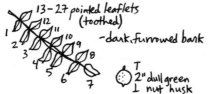

13-27 pointed leaflets (toothed)
- dark, furrowed bark
2" dull green nut husk

7 First-recorded street tree in Seattle (when counting trees in the right-of-way); also a Heritage Tree: 800 Hiawatha Pl. S., SW corner P-Patch, next to stairs; listed on January 1, 1950

Deodar Cedar
(CEDRUS DEODARA)

- dark furrowed bark, nearly black
1-2" needles on spurs in clusters
4" upright, round cone

8 Third-, fourth-, and fifth-widest diameter cedar street trees in District 3: 714 24th Ave. S.

English Maple
(ACER CAMPESTRE)

9 540 30th Ave. S., with abnormal trunk swelling caused by an unknown irritant

–twigs with "corky" ridges

3–5 lobes with <u>rounded</u> teeth

1   2

180°

1½" fruit with wide-spread wings

Trinity Pear
(PYRUS CALLERYANA 'TRINITY'

10 Fourth-recorded pear street trees in Seattle: 528 32nd Ave. S., a fruitless cultivar named 'Trinity' and listed August 1, 1976, the same day the Seattle Seahawks played their first-ever game at the newly constructed (now-demolished) Kingdome, against the San Francisco 49ers (Pears were once a popular street tree in the postwar suburbs, but their invasive tendencies became widely noticed by the 1990s and they are now being phased out)

2½" rounded leaf with wavy, toothed edge

white flowers with darker centers (March to April)

½" green fruit (if any)

Tulip Tree
(LIRIODENDRON TULIPIFERA)

11 Fourth-widest diameter tulip tree street tree in Seattle: 922 Davis Pl. S.

–green and orange flowers in June

5" leaf with four lobes

–gray, ridged bark with upside down "V" markings

Snow gum (*Eucalyptus pauciflora*)
7356 19th Ave. NW

LOYAL HEIGHTS Eucalyptus

Eucalyptus trees, native to Australia, arrived in California during the 1850s gold rush, where they were planted as "instant industrial forests" until it was discovered that the wood warped and cracked, making it commercially worthless. With the plantations in California long abandoned and eucalyptus now naturalized there, it has been called the state's "most hated tree" and is the subject of regular complaints citing everything from its flammable oil to pedestrian injuries caused by its falling bark.

By the 1930s, eucalyptus had made its way to the Pacific Northwest, but things didn't really take off until the mid-1970s. One tree had grown so well in the Washington Park Arboretum that in 1975 it became a source for the Colvos Creek Nursery's mail-order catalog, which shipped seedlings all across the United States until the nursery closed in 2014. But the best eucalyptus for our region were developed from specimens collected in the 1980s by University of Washington professor Stan Gessel in Australia, "on the upper slopes of Mt. Kosciusko in New South Wales," where snow covers the ground for part of the year and "freezing temperatures [are] likely to occur anytime." He grew these in front of his Maple Leaf home, where they are still thriving as Seattle's first-recorded eucalyptus street trees.

Loyal Heights—once a suburb of the independent city of Ballard— is now part of Seattle's District 6, which features the most eucalyptus street trees in the city (out of only 83 total!).

Eucalyptus

"the tree of purification"
EUCALYPTUS
EVERGREEN
Total: 83 *(0.04% of all right-of-way trees in Seattle)*

Cider Gum Eucalyptus
(EUCALYPTUS GUNNI)
Max Height: 120'

- Irregular shaped tree

2-6" leaf (dull, not glossy)

- Strong fragrance

- round, silver juvenile leaves (1-2")

1-2"

- buds in groups of 3

- brownish-orange bark flaking off to reveal smooth green

FROM AUSTRALIA

1 7012 18th Ave. NW; listed only as "*Eucalyptus sp.*"

2 Tied for second-widest diameter eucalyptus street tree in Seattle: 7338 26th Ave. NW

Snow Gum Eucalyptus
(EUCALYPTUS PAUCIFLORA)
Max Height: 82'

- leaning tree with short trunk

3-6" leaf (very thick, glossy; veins run parallel)

- weak fragrance

- buds in clusters of 7-12

- smooth whitish bark, multi-colored stripes or mottled shades

FROM AUSTRALIA

3 Seventh-widest diameter eucalyptus street tree in Seattle: 7356 19th Ave. NW

4 Tied as second- and third-widest diameter eucalyptus street trees in Seattle: 8041 13th Ave. NW; two with unusually large seeds

5 6728 Jones Ave. NW; listed only as "*Eucalyptus sp.*"

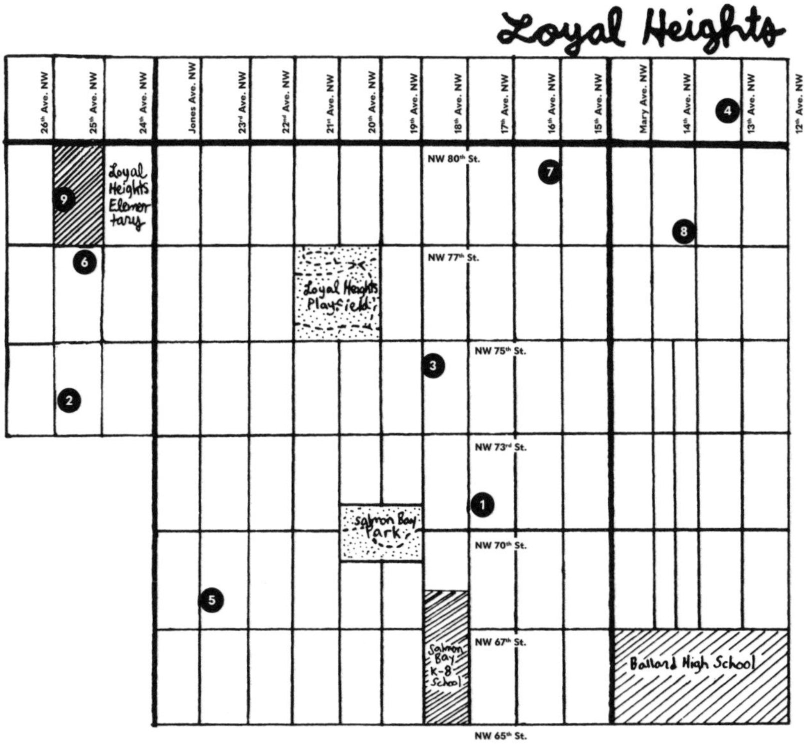

Loyal Heights

Street labels (top, left to right): 26th Ave. NW, 25th Ave. NW, 24th Ave. NW, Jones Ave. NW, 23rd Ave. NW, 22nd Ave. NW, 21st Ave. NW, 20th Ave. NW, 19th Ave. NW, 18th Ave. NW, 17th Ave. NW, 16th Ave. NW, 15th Ave. NW, Mary Ave. NW, 14th Ave. NW, 13th Ave. NW, 12th Ave. NW

NW 80th St.
NW 77th St.
NW 75th St.
NW 73rd St.
NW 70th St.
NW 67th St.
NW 65th St.

Loyal Heights Elementary
Loyal Heights Playfield
Salmon Bay Park
Salmon Bay K-8 School
Ballard High School

Also see:

- **Widest diameter eucalyptus street tree in Seattle:** Wallingford, cider gum (4228 Eastern Ave. N.)
- **Tied for eighth-widest diameter eucalyptus street tree in Seattle:** Phinney Ridge, snow gum (6056 4th Ave. NW)
- **10th-widest diameter eucalyptus street tree in Seattle:** Green Lake, atypical cider gum (5642 Keystone Pl. N.)
- **First-recorded eucalyptus street trees in Seattle:** Maple Leaf, snow gum (8514 Latona Ave. NE)

113

other notable Loyal Heights street trees:

Bolleana White Poplar
(POPULUS ALBA 'PYRAMIDAL

6 Second-widest diameter poplar street tree in Seattle: 7557 25th Ave. NW (on NW 77th St.); listed incorrectly in the city's data as "black cottonwood (*Populus balsamifera sp. trichocarpa*)"

3"

wavy edge

3-5 lobes

(white underside)

whitish bark, furrowed and darker on lower trunk

Black Locust
(ROBINIA PSEUDOACACIA)

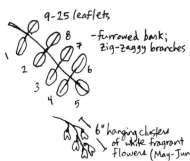

9-25 leaflets

—furrowed bark; zig-zaggy branches

6" hanging clusters of white fragrant flowers (May-June)

7 Tied for fourth-widest diameter black locust street tree in Seattle: 7733 16th Ave. NW

8 Seattle's only black locust Heritage Tree street tree: 7701 14th Ave. NW

Dawn Redwood
(METASEQUOIA GLYPHTOSTROBOIDES)

9 Second-widest diameter dawn redwood street trees in the city: 2501 NW 80th St. (west side of Loyal Heights Elementary); the widest dawn redwood street tree is in East Queen Anne at 1820 Warren Ave N.

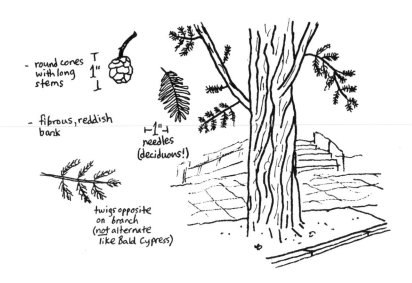

- round cones with long stems

1"

- fibrous, reddish bark

⊢1"⊣ needles (deciduous!)

twigs opposite on branch (not alternate like Bald Cypress)

MADISON &
WASHINGTON PARKS
Hawthorn

Known for its ability to live over 400 years and its distinctive thorny mass of twigs that creates an impenetrable hedge in all seasons, common hawthorn was introduced to the West Coast starting in the 1800s in Oregon and southern Washington. It took no time adapting to the Pacific Northwest and by the 1920s, it was practically naturalized, having established itself along dirt roadsides.

In 1929, a Seattle parking-strip committee, calling itself Plant a Tree, announced that "after considering the growth of various trees above and below ground," it recommended hawthorn as the most suitable tree for curb plantings. The committee's advice may have been heeded, as today hawthorn is the city's fourth-most abundant street tree with over 7,000 total, responsible for annually removing one million pounds of carbon dioxide from our atmosphere. From May to June, the city's streets are decked out with the hawthorn's white (and sometimes pink or red!) blossoms.

District 3, which includes Madison Park and Washington Park, has the most hawthorn street trees in the city. The area was called "Where One Chops" by the Duwamish peoples who originally lived there. Later, the first white settler in the area, Judge John McGilvra, had a road cut from the lake to downtown in 1864, creating modern-day Madison Street. A cable car line was added in 1890, and cross-lake ferry service shortly thereafter, making Madison Park a pleasure destination (even more so after the water level of the lake was lowered in 1917). The cable car and ferries are long gone, but the beach continues to draw crowds (by bus and car), and Madison Street is still a main thoroughfare.

English midland hawthorn (*Crataegus laevigata*)
3702 E. Highland Dr.

Hawthorn "the tree of contradictions"

CRATAEGUS
DECIDUOUS
Total: 7,083 (4% of all right-of-way trees in Seattle)

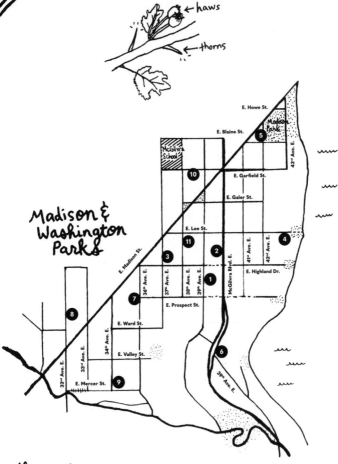

← haws

← thorns

Madison & Washington Parks

Also see:

- **Third-widest diameter hawthorn street tree in Seattle:** Beacon Hill, English midland hawthorn (3230 Lafayette Ave. S.)
- **First-recorded hawthorn street trees in Seattle:** West Seattle, English midland (Fauntleroy) (3531 SW Monroe St.)

Carrière Hawthorn
(CRATAEGUS X LAVALLEI)
Max Height: 40'

- grayish bark, scaly; twisted, burly trunk with dense twigs

2" barely lobed leaf; thick and glossy (sheds late winter, nearly evergreen)

- may have a few thorns on branches

3/4" orange fruit

May to June: white flowers, 5 petals, unpleasant fragrance

HYBRIDIZED IN FRANCE

1 1126 39th Ave. NE

2 **Tied as widest diameter hawthorn street tree in Washington Park/ Madison Park: 1225 McGilvra Blvd.**

Common Hawthorn
(CRATAEGUS MONOGYNA)
Max Height: 70'

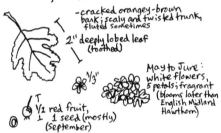

- cracked orangey-brown bark; scaly and twisted trunk, fluted sometimes

2" deeply lobed leaf (toothed)

1/3"

May to June: white flowers, 5 petals; fragrant (blooms later than English Midland Hawthorn)

1/2 red fruit, 1 seed (mostly) (September)

FROM EUROPE, S. AFRICA

3 **Tied as widest diameter hawthorn street tree in Washington Park/Madison Park: 3702 E. Highland Dr. (on 37th Ave. E.)**

4 4235 E. Lee St., two between a red maple and chestnut

English Midland Hawthorn
(CRATAEGUS LAEVIGATA)
Max Height: 40'

- similar bark/trunk as common Hawthorn

2" leaf, less lobed than common Hawthorn

May to June: pinkish-red flowers, often with 10+ petals, very fragrant (blooms earlier than common Hawthorn)

1/2" red fruit, 2-3 seeds

FROM EUROPE, W. AFRICA, W. ASIA

5 1803 42nd Ave. E.

6 800 McGilvra Blvd. E.

other notable street trees :

English Elm
(ULMUS PROCERA)

4" roundish, crumpled leaf
(double-toothed)

1" papery seeds

"corky" grooved twigs

7 Tied as ninth-widest diameter elm street trees in Seattle: 1039 and 1101 36th Ave. E., listed incorrectly in city's data as American Elm (some real American elms on 37th Ave. E.)

Common Horse Chestnut
(AESCULUS HIPPOCASTANUM)

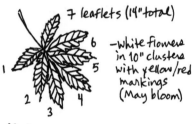

7 leaflets (14" total)

—white flowers in 10" clusters with yellow/red markings (May bloom)

8 Tied for widest diameter horse chestnut street tree in Seattle: 1016 32nd Ave. E., also a Heritage Tree

Katsura
(CERCIDIPHYLLUM JAPONICUM)

—grayish bark

3" round/heart-shaped leaf (bluntly-toothed) (brilliant yellow and orange late-September to October)

♂ small red tufts of flowers (March)

♀ 3/4" pods (October)

9 Widest diameter katsura street tree in District 3: 614 34th Ave. E.

Tulip Tree
(LIRIODENDRON TULIPFERA)

5" leaf with 4 lobes

—green and orange flowers in June

gray, ridged bark with upside-down "V" markings

10 Seventh-widest diameter tulip tree street tree in Seattle: 3815 E. Garfield St.

Western Red Cedar
(THUJA PLICATA)

- reddish, fibrous bark, often fluted and buttressed
- scaly foliage

1/3" cone with toothed scale tips

⓫ Only street in Seattle lined with western red cedars: 38th Ave. E., south of E. Lee St. (also around the corner on E. Lee St., west of 38th Ave. E.) with widest at 1228 38th Ave. E.

DENNY-BLAINE/
MADISON VALLEY
False Cypress

True cypress trees have been long revered as symbols of eternity and timelessness in ancient Mediterranean countries, but few are planted as street trees in Seattle.

Washington's native "false" cypress, confusingly named Alaska cedar, was reported in 1900 to have been "not much logged yet, since it is rather hard to get at." Perhaps our most familiar false cypress though is the Lawson cypress, native to nearby coastal Oregon and Northern California. In the 1920s, it was heavily planted in and around Seattle, until the discovery of cypress root rot. Sixty percent of coastal second-growth Lawson cypress planted after 1930 was lost to the disease; to date, there is no known cure, although there are still around 1,200 false cypress street trees remaining in Seattle.

District 3, which encompasses Madison Valley and Denny-Blaine, has the fourth-most false cypress right-of-way trees in the city, while there is not a single true cypress street tree east of 23rd Street. Madison Valley was established largely by William Grose, one of the first Black settlers in Seattle and the owner of the popular three-story Pioneer Square restaurant/hotel called Our House. When Our House burned down in the Great Seattle Fire of 1889, Grose and his family moved out to a wooded 12-acre farm in a valley a few miles away, which he had purchased from mill owner Henry Yesler. At the time, the area was unpaved, with streets winding through "fallen trees, stumps and underbrush." One of the few neighborhoods that didn't prevent Black Americans from buying homes, by 1950 it had the largest concentration of Black homeowners in the city.

Sawara cypress (*Chamaecyparis pisifera*)
431 31st Ave. E.

CUPRESSUS & CHAMAECYPARIS

EVERGREEN

Total: 1,244 (0.7% of all right-of-way trees in Seattle)
false

Total: 189 (0.1% of all right-of-way trees in Seattle)
true

True and False Cypress

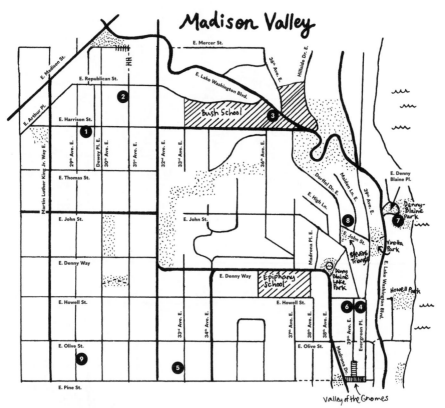

Madison Valley

Leyland Cypress
(CUPRESSUS X LEYLANDII)
Max Height: 120'

scale-like foliage
in sprays at all angles
around twigs

"beak" → round cones
rarely produced

HYBRIDIZED IN THE UK

1 Only known true cypress street tree in this neighborhood: 2917 E. Harrison St., a street tree missing from the city's data

Lawson Cypress
(CHAMAECYPARIS
Max Height: 245'
(from SW Oregon to NW California)

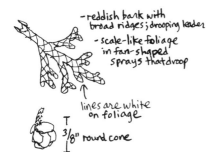

- reddish bark with broad ridges; drooping leader
- scale-like foliage in fan-shaped sprays that droop

lines are white on foliage

T ⊥ 3/8" round cone

Italian Cypress
(CUPRESSUS SEMPERVIRENS)
Max Height: 164'

scaly foliage radiating in all directions from branch

- rough, fibrous bark

- wide-spreading in natural form, or "flame-shaped" if pruned

T ⊥ 1 1/3" round "cone"

Sawara Cypress
(CHAMAECYPARIS PISIFERA)
Max Height: 164'

- stringy bark; open and sparse
- Prickly curling foliage, yellowish and soft
(foliage thins over time)

FROM JAPAN

2 431 31st Ave. E., a pair next to a Western red cedar

3 Lake Washington Blvd., east of E. Republican St. and west of 36th Ave. E: south side, in right-of-way just south of the entrance sign to the Bush School

- **Widest diameter *true* cypress street tree in Seattle:** Ravenna, Italian cypress (7051 Ravenna Ave. NE)
- **Second-widest diameter false cypress street tree in Seattle:** Ballard, sawara cypress (3048 NW 60th St.)
- **Third-widest diameter false cypress street tree in Seattle:** Cherry Hill, Lawson cypress (2120 E. Fir St.)
- **Fourth-widest diameter false cypress street tree in Seattle:** University District, Lawson cypress (4722 18th Ave. NE)
- **Fifth-widest diameter false cypress street tree in Seattle:** Beacon Hill, lawson cypress (1602 S. Hill St.)
- **Sixth-widest diameter false cypress street tree in Seattle:** University District, sawara cypress (1724 NE 55th St.)

other notable street trees:

Coast Redwood
(SEQUOIA SEMPERVIRENS)

1" needles in feathery, flat sprays

yellowish pollen cones at twig tips

— reddish, fibrous bark

1" cone

④ Third-widest diameter coast redwood street tree in Seattle (when including right-of-way trees): 3909 E. Howell St., at corner

English Walnut
(JUGLANS REGIA)

7-9 broad leaflets with leaf at tip the widest

— smooth-ridged grayish bark

2 1/2" nut

⑤ Fourth-widest diameter English walnut street tree in Seattle: 1607 33rd Ave.

European Beech
(FAGUS SYLVATICA)

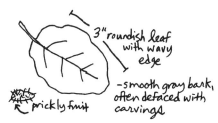

3" roundish leaf with wavy edge

—smooth gray bark, often defaced with carvings

prickly fruit

6 **Widest diameter beech street tree in Seattle: 1733 39th Ave.**

Littleleaf Linden
(TILIA CORDATA)

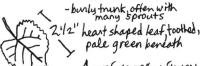

- burly trunk, often with many sprouts

2 1/2" heart shaped leaf, toothed, pale green beneath

profuse yellow flowers in June; fragrant

7 **City's widest diameter linden right-of-way tree: 4021 E. Denny-Blaine Pl., south border of Denny-Blaine Park (Seattle's unofficial nude beach), with several smaller bigleaf linden in the parking circle**

Deodar Cedar
(CEDRUS DEODARA)

—drooping branches, multiple trunks

1-2" needles on spurs in clusters

4" upright, round cone

8 **Tied for second-widest diameter cedar street tree in the city: 218 Dorffel Dr. E., intersection of E. John St. and Maiden Lane at northern tip of Stevens Triangle; listed in city's data on January 1, 1951, the day the University of Washington took possession of what was then known as the Seattle Repertory Playhouse due to its founders being investigated by the Washington State Legislative Fact-finding Committee on Un-American Activities**

Pacific Madrona
(ARBUTUS MENZIESII)

—reddish peeling bark, gnarled, leaning tree

4" leathery leaf

3/8" red berries (October)

urn-shaped white flowers (March-May)

9 **Third-widest diameter madrona street tree in Seattle: 1618 29th Ave.**

Western red cedar (*Thuja plicata*)
527 30th Ave.

MADRONA
Arborvitae

While there are 653 American arborvitae street trees in Seattle, the best-known species is not called an "arborvitae" at all. Our confusingly named "western red cedar" is considered one of the most sacred trees of indigenous peoples in the region.

Upon visiting the Pacific Northwest for the first time in the late 1830s, explorer Charles Wilkes wrote of the "gigantic fine cedar forest," saying he "could not control" his astonishment at the size of the giants. More recently, beginning in 2015, western red cedars in urban corridors have begun inexplicably dying. "There's no pattern to it," observed a property owner quoted in a 2022 *Seattle Times* article. Many scientists believe it is climate-related. In the past 20 years, Washington has experienced seven of its 10 hottest years since 1895, and while western red cedar can normally survive a seasonal drought or a single heat wave, multiple weather events in quick succession deprive it of adequate time to recover.

Overall, there are 1,620 western red cedar right-of-way trees in Seattle, making up the majority of our arborvitae and responsible for annually removing one million pounds of carbon dioxide from our atmosphere. District 3, where Madrona is located, has the least. Madrona was where the first chapter of the Black Panther Party outside California was begun in 1968, in an old storefront that still exists today. After being targeted by the police, the headquarters was moved to a house on 20th Avenue, where they eventually disbanded in 1978 after establishing the Carolyn Downs Family Medical Center— the first free medical clinic in the Pacific Northwest—which continues to operate today on Yesler Way.

Arborvitae "the tree of life"
THUJA
EVERGREEN
Total: 2,410 (1.4% of all right-of-way trees in Seattle)

American Arborvitae
(THUJA OCCIDENTALIS)
Max Height: 125'

FROM EASTERN N. AMERICA

1 3010 E. Spruce St.

- grayish-brown fibrous bark; slow-growing

- lacy scale-like foliage in flat fan-shaped sprays (underside same color, no white markings like Western Red Cedar)

½" upright cone

Western Red Cedar
(THUJA PLICATA)
Max Height: 130'

NATIVE FROM S. ALASKA TO N. CALIFORNIA

- reddish fibrous bark; often fluted and buttressed with elbow-like branches and an erect leader

- lacy scale-like foliage

faint whitish "butterfly" pattern on underside of foliage

⅓" upright cone with toothed scale tips

2 Widest diameter arborvitae street tree in Seattle: 1136 35th Ave. (on E. Union St.)

3 Sixth-widest diameter arborvitae street tree in Seattle: 805 27th Ave.

4 Third-widest diameter arborvitae street tree in District 3: 527 30th Ave.

5 Fourth-widest diameter arborvitae street tree in District 3: 2606 E. Spring St.

6 932 27th Ave., a pair

7 718 27th Ave.

8 313 32nd Ave., several

Madrona

E. Union St.

E. Spring St.

E. Marion St.

E. Columbia St.

E. Cherry St.

E. James St.

E. Jefferson St.

E. Terrace St.

E. Alder St.

E. Spruce St.

E. Yesler Way

27th Ave.

Martin Luther King Jr. Way

29th Ave.

30th Ave.

31st Ave.

32nd Ave.

33rd Ave.

34th Ave.

35th Ave.

36th Ave.

Madrona Elementary

Madrona Playground

St. Therese Academy

Powell Barnett Park

Leschi Elementary

Also see:

- **Second-widest diameter arborvitae street tree in Seattle:** Columbia City, western red cedar (4431 S. Brandon St.)
- **Tied as third-widest diameter arborvitae street tree in Seattle:** Wallingford, western red cedar (4515 Woodlawn Ave. N.) and West Seattle (4403 SW Seattle St.)
- **Tied for fifth-widest diameter arborvitae street tree in Seattle:** NW Queen Anne, western red cedar (1007 Raye St. and 22 Howe St.)
- **Widest of Seattle's only street lined with western red cedars:** Washington Park (1228 38th Ave. E.)
- **Widest diameter American arborvitae street tree in Seattle:** *Not illustrated:* Hillman City (3302 S. Orcas St.)
- **First-recorded western red cedar street tree in Seattle:** Magnolia (2720 W. Galer St.)
- **Second-recorded western red cedar street tree in Seattle:** Capitol Hill (1508 E. Prospect St.)

MADRONA
other notable street trees:

American Sycamore
(PLATANUS OCCIDENTALIS)

- finely checkered bark
- 3-5 lobed leaf (7")
- ←long stalk
- 1¼" seed balls (hanging <u>singly</u>)

9 Widest diameter American sycamore street tree in Seattle: 128 30th Ave.

American Basswood Linden
(TILIA AMERICANA)

7" or more; lopsided leaf (not fuzzy beneath)

Fragrant yellow flowers in June

10 Seventh-widest diameter linden street tree in Seattle: 415 35th Ave., at road end (with a bigleaf linden at the corner next to fire hydrant)

Black Locust
(ROBINIA PSEUDOACACIA)

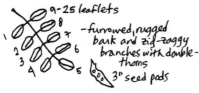

9-25 leaflets

- furrowed, rugged bark and zig-zaggy branches with double-thorns
- 3" seed pods

11 Tied as third-widest diameter black locust street tree in Seattle: 1133 35th Ave.

Ponderosa Pine
(PINUS PONDEROSA)
Max height: 300'

5-11"

-3-6" prickly cones; reddish

- needles in bundles of 3
- orange, furrowed and plated bark

12 1118 29th Ave.: widest of the ponderosa street trees planted experimentally on these four blocks in the 1970s (a western white pine nearby at 910 27th Ave. is the third-widest pine street tree in city)

Douglas Fir
(PSEUDOTSUGA MENZIESII)

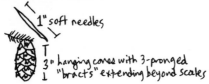

1" soft needles

3" hanging cones with 3-pronged "bracts" extending beyond scales

13 Fourth-widest diameter Douglas fir street tree in Seattle: 528 30th Ave.

American basswood linden (*Tilia americana*)
415 35th Ave.

MAGNOLIA
Magnolia

The magnolia tree has been found in fossils dating back 100 million years ago, making it the first known flowering plant. This didn't matter in 1908 Seattle when "a mature person who knew perfectly well what he was doing" cut two feet off the top of one of S. P. Hicks's seven-foot-tall magnolia street trees, which he had imported and maintained at his own expense. The *Seattle Daily Times* subtitled the story it printed "Person Unknown to Police Cuts Top of Beautiful Magnolia Tree in Parking Strip, and Owner Wants Protection." The article stated that "malicious destruction and mutilation" of trees in parking strips had become a frequent occurrence in the city.

Magnolias were a hot commodity in Seattle apparently. In 1927, C. P. Dana of Columbia City boasted that his 12-foot-tall magnolia tree had produced 75 blooms. The *Seattle Daily Times* reported that his magnolia was "said to be only one of three ever successfully grown in the Northwest." Crawford E. White, a Mount Baker attorney, decided to enter the best-magnolia fray in 1936, claiming that his 12-foot magnolia tree had produced 185 blooms the previous year. By 1950, White bragged that the same tree was now 30 feet tall and produced about 450 blooms each summer, allowing him "to pick from one to ten blossoms a day."

Seafaring European explorers named Seattle's Magnolia neighborhood after mistakenly thinking they saw magnolia trees dotting the bluff. What they had actually seen were Pacific madronas, but the neighborhood still took great pride in its namesake, decidedly owning it by deliberately planting the most magnolia street trees in the entire city.

Samuel Sommer evergreen magnolia (*Magnolia grandiflora* 'Samuel Sommer')
3211 McGraw St.

Magnolia

"the tree of magnificence"

MAGNOLIA

Total: 3,112 (1.8% of all right-of-way trees in Seattle)

Evergreen Magnolia
(MAGNOLIA GRANDIFLORA)
Max Height: 147'

-pyrimadal tree with smooth gray bark and dense foliage

6-11" leaves; glossy, leathery with brown fuzz underneath

3" fruit
late May bloom →

10"+ fragrant white flowers
(6-12 "tepals")

EVERGREEN • FROM EASTERN UNITED STATES

1 Fifth-widest diameter magnolia street trees in Seattle: 3204 and 3220 W. McGraw St., a cultivar called 'Samuel Sommer'

2 First-recorded magnolia street tree in Seattle: 1801 30th Ave. W., listed on September 9, 1970, the same day 60 people were arrested at a "fish in" on the Puyallup River practicing Native American treaty fishing rights

Cucumber Magnolia
(MAGNOLIA ACUMINATA)
Max Height: 141'

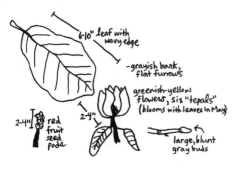

6-10" leaf with wavy edge

-grayish bark, flat furrows

greenish-yellow flowers, six "tepals" (blooms with leaves in May)

2-4" red fruit seed pods

2-4"

large, blunt gray buds

DECIDUOUS • FROM EASTERN UNITED STATES

3 Seattle's only known Cucumber Magnolia street tree: 1811 29th Ave. W., originally listed as "saucer magnolia" in city's data

Galaxy Magnolia
(MAGNOLIA LILIIFLORA 'NIGRA' x SPRENGERI 'DIVA')
Max Height: 40'

-single-trunked, upright tree

10" purplish flowers (11-12 "tepals") (late April bloom)

greenish, slender buds

DECIDUOUS • HYBRIDIZED IN THE UNITED STATES, 1980s

4 Tied as third-widest diameter magnolia street tree in Seattle: 3607 W. 34th Ave. W., a hybrid released in 1980

Magnolia

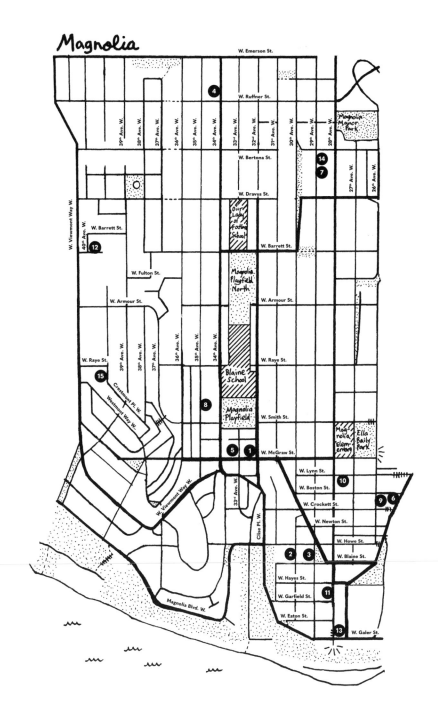

Hybrid Kobus Magnolia
(MAGNOLIA X LOEBNERI)
Max Height: 46'

4-6" flowers in April
(11-15 floppy, narrow "tepals")
white (sometimes pale pink)

DECIDUOUS • FROM JAPAN, S. KOREA

⑤ 3300 W. McGraw St., wrapping around onto 33rd Ave. W., listed in city's data as Kobus Magnolia (however Kobus have only six petals and bloom later in April)

Saucer Magnolia
(MAGNOLIA X SOULANGEANA)
Max Height: 51'

- shrubby, spreading tree
5" leaves; stiff, arched with wavy edge
~ 1" blunt, silky buds
7½" flowers, white with purple or pink stripes (9 "tepals")
(March/April through August)

DECIDUOUS • HYBRIDIZED IN PARIS, 1800s

⑥ Second-widest diameter saucer magnolia street tree in Seattle: 2106 W. Boston St. (illustrated on the right)

⑦ 3222 29th Ave. W., small young street trees

Sweetbay Magnolia
(MAGNOLIA VIRGINIANA)
Max Height: 95'

- often a crooked, forked tree
4" leaves with very pale undersides (aromatic when crushed)
blunt pointed
fragrant
2-4" white flowers (9-12 "tepals")
(June-July)

SEMI-EVERGREEN • FROM EASTERN UNITED STATES

⑧ Only sweetbay magnolia street trees in Magnolia: 2542 35th Ave. W., a very young pair planted right before the pandemic in 2019

Yellow Magnolia
(MAGNOLIA 'BUTTERFLIES')

tulip shape
4-5" yellow flowers appear before leaves, upright with 10-16 "tepals" (instead of petals)

DECIDUOUS • PATENTED IN 1991 IN THE UNITED STATES

⑨ Only yellow magnolia street trees in Magnolia: 2106 26th Ave. W., small young trees

Also see:

- **Tied as widest and third-widest diameter magnolia street trees in Seattle:** Georgetown, evergreen magnolia (222 S. Orcas St.)
- **Second-widest diameter magnolia street tree in Seattle:** *Not illustrated:* Wallingford, evergreen magnolia (4014 Midvale Ave. N.)
- **Fourth-widest diameter magnolia street tree in Seattle:** North Beacon Hill, evergreen magnolia (1901 S. Plum St. traffic circle); *Not illustrated:* North Magnolia, evergreen magnolia (4333 32nd Ave. W.)
- **Widest saucer magnolia in Seattle (also tied as sixth-widest diameter magnolia street tree in city overall):** Ravenna (1308 NE 62nd St.)

MAGNOLIA
other notable street trees:

Japanese Maple
(ACER PALMATUM)

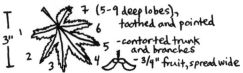

7 (5-9 deep lobes), toothed and pointed
-contorted trunk and branches
3/4" fruit, spread wide

10 Widest diameter and first recorded Japanese maple street tree in Seattle: 2645 W. Lynn St.; listed September 6, 1950

Deodar Cedar
(CEDRUS DEODARA)

1-2" needles on spurs in clusters
4" upright, round cone

11 Fourth-widest cedar street tree in Seattle: 1611 28th Ave. W.; listed on September 9, 1950

Douglas Fir
(PSEUDOTSUGA MENZIESII)

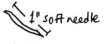

1" soft needle

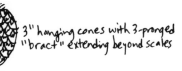

3" hanging cones with 3-pronged "bract" extending beyond scales

12 Widest Douglas fir street tree in Seattle: 3939 W. Barrett St., (where 40th Ave. W. and W. Barrett Ln. meet) in median with a road sign on it

Western Red Cedar
(THUJA PLICATA)

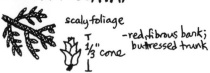

scaly foliage
-red, fibrous bark; buttressed trunk
1/3" cone

13 First-recorded street trees in District 7: 2720 W. Galer St., flanking corner steps, two incorrectly listed in city's data as "Lawson cypress" on August 13, 1950—during Seattle's first-ever Seafair festival; the annual gala has continued for over 70 years, canceled only once in 2020.

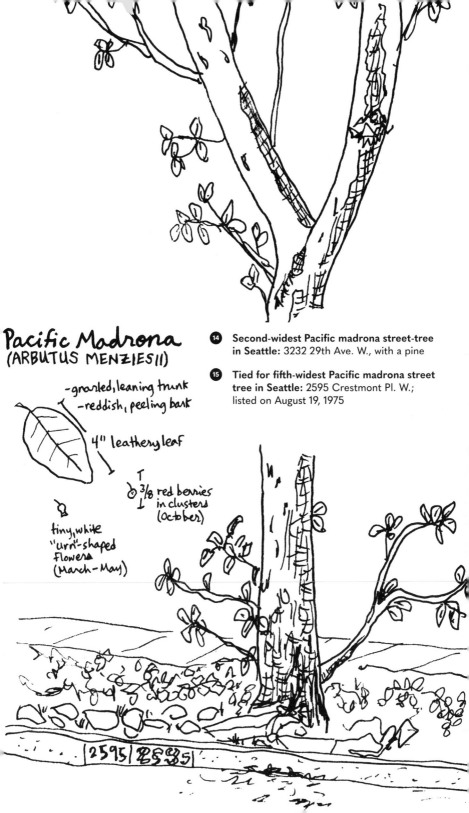

Pacific Madrona
(ARBUTUS MENZIESII)

- gnarled, leaning trunk
- reddish, peeling bark

4" leathery leaf

3/8 red berries in clusters (October)

tiny, white "urn"-shaped flowers (March–May)

14 Second-widest Pacific madrona street-tree in Seattle: 3232 29th Ave. W., with a pine

15 Tied for fifth-widest Pacific madrona street tree in Seattle: 2595 Crestmont Pl. W.; listed on August 19, 1975

2595

Lombardy poplar (*Populus nigra* 'Italica')
1752 NE 91st St.

MAPLE LEAF
Poplar

The word *poplar* comes from *populus,* the Latin word for *people,* and it was one of the first trees historically used along roads. The oldest living organism on the planet is a poplar in Utah which actually looks like a stand of quaking aspen trees, except that its more than 40,000 trunks are all connected underground via the same root system spreading over 100 acres and thought to be at least 14,000 years old with some estimates suggesting almost a million years old. (The quaking aspen is uniquely capable of cloning itself and creating a forest all by itself, with each clone bearing the same DNA.)

Another popular poplar, the Lombardy poplar, cultivated in Italy, was first introduced to the United States around 1780, and was one of the most widely planted street trees for a generation of American towns. That is, until 1809, when New York City found that the partial failure of its water supply was due to poplar roots blocking pipes on Wall Street. By 1819, the citizens of New York had begun voluntarily removing them. Seattle chose not to heed the warning, though, and planted poplar street trees anyway. Nearly 200 years later, a city arborist confirmed: "They are terrible street trees."

Today, Seattle is home to the largest Lombardy poplars in the world outside of New Zealand.

District 5, which includes Maple Leaf, has the second-most poplar right-of-way trees in Seattle (out of a total of 940) and is home to a couple of the widest in diameter. Possibly named after the Maple Saw Mill on Lake Washington, Maple Leaf became home to the nation's first regional shopping center, the Northgate mall, in 1950.

poplar "the tree of eloquence"
POPULUS
DECIDUOUS
Total: 930 (0.5% of all right-of-way trees in Seattle)

maple Leaf

Also see:

- **Widest diameter poplar tree in Seattle's right-of-way (not in data):** South Park, Lombardy poplar (738 S. Sullivan St.)
- **Tied for widest diameter poplar street trees in Seattle:** Fremont, Bolleana poplar (3635 Fremont Ave. N.); Capitol Hill, Lombardy poplar (907 14th Ave. E.)
- **Second-widest diameter poplar street tree in Seattle:** Queen Anne, Lombardy poplar (222 Highland Dr.)
- **Third-widest diameter poplar street tree in Seattle:** Eastlake, Lombardy poplar (10 E. Roanoke St.)
- **Fourth-widest diameter poplar street tree in Seattle:** Loyal Heights, Bolleana poplar (7557 25th Ave. NW)
- **Sixth- and seventh-widest diameter poplar street trees in Seattle:** Georgetown, two Lombardy poplars (601 S. Brandon St.)
- **Eighth-widest diameter poplar street trees in Seattle:** *Not illustrated:* Capitol Hill, Lombardy poplar (803 E. Prospect St.)
- **Eighth-widest diameter poplar street tree in District 3:** Capitol Hill, Bolleana poplar (115 18th Ave. E.)
- **Seattle's only known railway poplars:** Mount Baker (Mount Baker Blvd., median east of 33rd Ave. S.)

Lombardy Poplar
(POPULUS NIGRA 'ITALICA')
Max Height: 157'

MALE CLONE ORIGINATING FROM ITALY, LATE 1600s

① **Fifth-widest diameter poplar street tree in Seattle:** 1752 NE 91st St., three

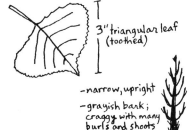

3" triangular leaf (toothed)

- narrow, upright
- grayish bark; craggy with many burls and shoots

Quaking Aspen
(POPULUS TREMULOIDES)
Max Height: 126'

FROM N. AMERICA

② 8118 4th Ave. NE

③ Sacajawea Park: 1726 NE 94th S., six by the fence on the north side

flat leafstalk

3" pointed, circular leaf (toothed)

- whitish bark; smooth, with black scars

- fuzzy catkins

White Poplar
(POPULUS ALBA)
Max Height: 140'

FROM N. AFRICA, W. ASIA

④ 1014 NE 88th St.: north side peeping over fence (*not a street tree but a great example of white poplar originally identified in* Trees of Seattle *by Arthur Lee Jacobson*)

3" leaf with 3-5 lobes (wavy edges)

- underleaf is white and fuzzy
- whitish bark becoming black and furrowed at base

- pointed fruit capsules

MAPLE LEAF
other notable street trees:

Black Locust
(ROBINIA PSEUDOACACIA)

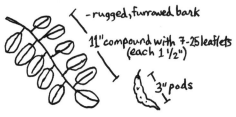

- rugged, furrowed bark

11" compound with 7-25 leaflets
(each 1 ½")

3" pods

⑤ Second-widest diameter street trees in Maple Leaf: 7802 Roosevelt Way NE (on NE 78th St.)

Pink Flowering Dogwood
(CORNUS FLORIDA F. RUBRA)

4 ½" leaf with veins parallel to edges

1
2
3
4 flower bracts (pink; April/May)
notched tip

⑥ First-recorded dogwood street trees in Seattle: 8513 4th Ave. NE; listed as eastern dogwood in city's data on August 18, 1970—the same day the *Seattle Daily Times* reported a petition to ban smoking on planes filed by consumer advocate Ralph Nader was rejected by federal court. Bans came 30 years later.

Mazzard Cherry
(PRUNUS AVIUM)

oval leaf, toothed edge
- white flowers
(mid-April)
bark with lines

⑦ Second-widest mazzard cherry street tree in Seattle: 819 NE 84th St.

Norway Spruce
(PICEA ABIES)

¾" rigid needles

- drooping twigs!

4-9" narrow cone (toothed scales)

⑧ Seattle's first-recorded spruce street tree (and Maple Leaf's first-recorded street tree overall): 8535 4th Ave. NE; listed in city's data only as "spruce" on July 25, 1970—the day before self-taught Seattle rock legend Jimi Hendrix would play his last hometown show at the old Sicks' Stadium (currently a Lowe's hardware store); he died in London less than two months later, at the age of 27.

Snow Gum Eucalyptus
(EUCALYPTUS PAUCIFLORA)

buds in clusters of 7-12

3-6" thick, glossy leaf with veins parallel to edges

9 First-recorded eucalyptus street trees in Seattle: 8514 Latona Ave. NE; listed only as "*Eucalyptus sp.*" in the city's data on July 25, 1978—the same day downtown Seattle's Rainier Club first admitted a Black member

-smooth whitish bark with multi-colored stripes and mottling

Littleleaf linden (*Tilia cordata*)
3337 Hunter Blvd. S.

MOUNT BAKER
Linden

In the summer, the tiny flowers of lindens (also called "lime trees" in European countries) perfume the air, reputed to be anxiolytic and intoxicating. Perhaps it is this calming, hypnotic effect associated with the tree that made it ideal for gathering under for court hearings. Northern Germanic tribes from the fourth century BC to the second century AD believed that hearings conducted under linden trees were blessed by the goddess of love, Freyja, who would ensure justice. This custom continued under the Holy Roman Empire when a linden was often planted in the center of each town as a place of assembly.

Long gone are the days of gathering under linden trees. In fact, a gardening columnist for the *Seattle Daily Times* warned specifically in 1962 that the trees "will drip hard-to-remove honey dew on automobiles parked under them." Far from being deemed sacred, lindens were described merely as "satisfactory to use, provided no car or lawn seat is to be left under them."

Today, there are roughly 4,300 linden right-of-way trees in Seattle, overall responsible for removing one million pounds of carbon dioxide from our atmosphere each year. The Mount Baker neighborhood is home to Hunter Boulevard, which has one of the city's densest concentrations of linden street trees. The neighborhood is also where the city's former pumphouse once operated, at present-day Mount Baker Park. During the Great Seattle Fire of 1889, water was pumped from Lake Washington through hollow log pipes to douse the flames in Pioneer Square. But the supply was not adequate, and the fire was devastating, leading the city to choose the Cedar River as its future water source.

"the tree of love"
TILIA
DECIDUOUS
Total: 4,299 (2.5% of all right-of-way trees in Seattle)

Bigleaf Linden
(TILIA PLATYPHYLLOS)
Max Height: 96'

2" —rounded crown; graying with interlaced ridges

6" heart-shaped leaf; fuzzy underneath (toothed)

½" first of Lindens to flower (June); 3-6 per bract, fragrant

FROM EUROPE, SW ASIA

1 Across from 3245 Hunter Blvd S., a tree on west side of median, between northern footpaths (with 18 others); listed incorrectly in city's data as littleleaf linden

Littleleaf Linden
(TILIA CORDATA)
Max Height: 96'

- older trees may be burly and with many trunk sprouts

2'½" heart-shaped leaf, pale green underneath (toothed)

June: fragrant, profuse yellow flowers (smaller fruit than Bigleaf) 5-11 per bract

FROM EUROPE, CAUCUSES

2 Across from 3337 Hunter Blvd. S., trees flanking benches between southern footpaths (with 36 others)

3 Across from 3242 Hunter Blvd. S., a leaning tree north of northern footpath, on east side of median

White Basswood
(TILIA HETEROPHYLLA)
Max Height: 135'

7-12' heart-shaped, lopsided leaf (toothed) hairy whitish underside

June fragrant yellow flowers become round "nuts" in fall (very few flowers)

FROM EASTERN N. AMERICA

4 Across from church at 3201 Hunter Blvd S., first three trees south of S. Hanford St. on west side of median (two trees south of them are more drought-resistant Silver Linden with fuzzy whitish leaf undersides)

Crimean Linden
(TILIA X EUCHLORA)
Max Height: 70'

- bright green-yellow twigs

3" heart-shaped shiny leaf (toothed)

flowers later than other lindens

FROM CRIMEA, CAUCUSES

5 Across from 3403 Hunter Blvd. S., tree on west side of median, immediately south of southern footpath (three others scattered here); listed incorrectly as littleleaf linden

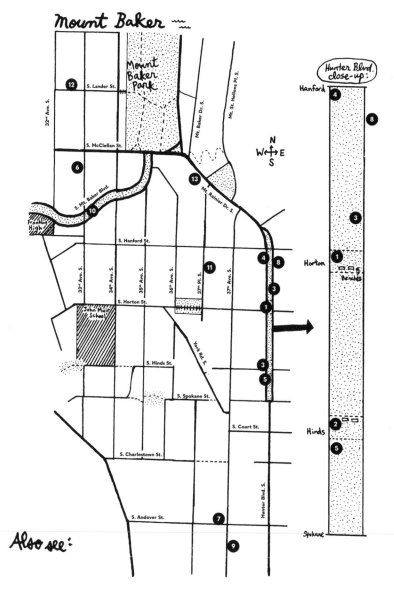

Mount Baker

- **Widest diameter linden street tree in Seattle:** Denny-Blaine, littleleaf linden (4021 E. Denny-Blaine Pl.)
- **Third-widest diameter linden street tree in Seattle:** Phinney Ridge, American basswood (133 N. 50th St.)
- **Seventh-widest diameter linden street tree in Seattle:** Madrona, American basswood (416 35th Ave.)
- **First-recorded linden street tree in Seattle:** Queen Anne, American basswood (520 W. Raye St.)

MOUNT BAKER
other notable street trees :

American White Elm
(ULMUS AMERICANA)

5" leaf (double-toothed)

T ½ seed

6 Mount Baker's second-widest diameter street tree: 2827 33rd Ave. S.

Bigleaf Maple
(ACER MACROPHYLLUM)

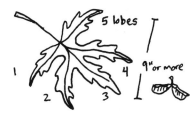

5 lobes

1 2 3 4

9" or more

7 Mount Baker's widest diameter maple street tree: 3859 37th Ave. S. (on S. Andover St.)

Giant Sequoia
(SEQUOIADENDRON GIGANTEUM)

–cord-like twigs

–reddish, fibrous bark

2 ½" cone

8 First-recorded giant sequoia street tree in Seattle (when including right-of-way trees): 3220 Hunter Blvd. S., bordering yard; listed on January 1, 1958—the day the European Union began (in 2020, the UK left)

Golden Weeping Willow
(SALIX 'CHRYSOCOMA')

–bright gold, flexible twigs

3–5" leaf (toothed)

weeping branches

9 Second-widest diameter willow street tree in Seattle: 4024 37th Ave. S.

Hybrid Black Poplar
(POPULUS X CANADENSIS)
'REGENERATA'

- makes "fluff" in summer (May-June)
- 4"
- tall, narrow, upright

10 Seattle's only known "railway poplars": Mount Baker Blvd., east of 33rd Ave. S.: center median, two (rare female hybrid clone that arose around 1814 in France and was once used widely in England beside railways; unlike the male Lombardy poplar, it produces fluffy white seeds May to June)

London Plane
(PLATANUS X ACERIFOLIA)

- shorter stalk than maples
- swollen trunk
- 3-5 lobes (toothed)
- 2 seed balls per stalk

11 Mount Baker's widest diameter street tree: 3232 37th Pl. S.

Southern Catalpa
(CATALPA BIGNONIOIDES)
'NANA'

- 10" seed pod
- 7" heart shaped leaf
- 2"
- bell-shaped flower

12 Mount Baker's widest diameter catalpa street trees: 3210 S. Lander St., a flowerless cultivar called umbrella catalpa

Tulip Tree
(LIRIODENDRON TULIPIFERA)

- green and orange flowers in June
- 5" leaf with four lobes
- gray, ridged bark with upside down "V" markings

13 Mount Baker's widest diameter tulip tree street tree: 2851 Mt. Rainier Dr. S.

PHINNEY RIDGE
cedar

Deodar cedar has been planted in the Pacific Northwest since seeds were brought from California in the 1830s. The tree became a favorite tool of civic-minded Seattle women; in 1930, the Evergreen Club announced that it would be planting 40 deodar cedars on what it called a "Recognition Lane" at Sand Point Naval Air Base.

"These trees will form a double line from the main entrance to the station, standing about thirty feet apart on either side of the avenue," the *Seattle Daily Times* reported. Under the direction of club president Mrs. George Adrian Smith, an early-day leader of the Pacific Northwest suffragist movement, a Mrs. F. W Hargrave supervised the project and was the original person who thought of planting the trees in a line. It was her vision that the row of deodar cedars would "in time rival the famous avenue of these trees in Pasadena." While the club originally said the trees would honor both women and men, the cedars of Recognition Lane were largely dedicated to living female leaders. Nearly a century later, many of those cedars remain.

Deodar cedars were famous for something else in Seattle too: By the 1940s, they dominated the winning entries for Seattle's annual Outdoor Lighted Christmas Tree Contest. However, it was said to be "difficult to deck this kind of tree with lights because the branches are so pliant."

There are 500 true cedar street trees in Seattle, and Phinney Ridge is home to two of the widest diameter deodar cedar street trees in the city. Phinney Ridge was named after developer Guy Phinney, who built his English-style manor here, with a formal rose garden and menagerie. Today it has become the Woodland Park Zoo.

Deodar cedar (*Cedrus deodara*)
119 N. 49th St.

"the tree of strength"
CEDRUS
EVERGREEN
Total: 500 (0.3% of all right-of-way trees in Seattle)

Atlas Cedar
(CEDRUS ATLANTICA)
Max Height: 160'

- flat-topped tree
  (branches not drooping
  like Deodar cedar)
- 3/4" needles silvery-blue
  in bunches along branches
- cracked, grayish bark
- horizontal layers of foliage

Cones like Deodar Cedar
except smaller

FROM ATLAS MOUNTAINS, NW AFRICA

1 6056 4th Ave. NW (on NW
62nd St., west of a weeping
Atlas cedar street tree
and east of a snow gum
eucalyptus)

Deodar Cedar
(CEDRUS DEODARA)
Max Height: 250'

- grayish-black
  bark, furrowed
  and cracked; branches
  and leader droop; may
  have multiple trunks
- 1-2" needles
  on spurs in clusters

♀

4" cone (green then brown),
sits upright on branches;
falling apart in
layers over winter

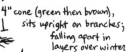

(trees can be
male, female,
or bisexual)

♂ male pollen
shed October
to December

FROM HIMALAYAS

2 **Tied for widest diameter
cedar street tree in Seattle:
611 N. 64th St.**

3 **Tied for widest diameter
cedar street tree in Seattle:
119 N. 49th St.;** according
to neighbors, this tree
was planted in the early
1900s, when the original
homeowner was selling oil
that a local family couldn't
afford during the epic
winter of 1910; a barter was
reached in which the family
planted the tree in exchange
for the fuel

Cedar of Lebanon
(CEDRUS LIBANI)

- foliage in level,
  horizontal
  layers
- 1" needles,
  silvery-blue
  in bunches
  along branches

upright, round
cone

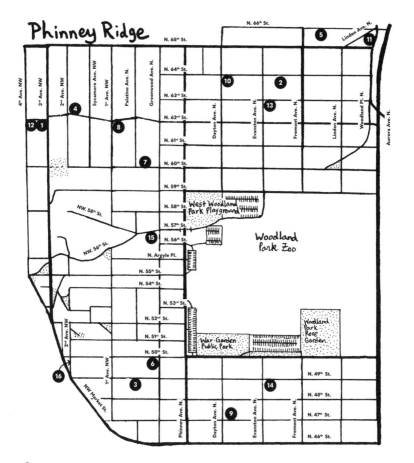

Phinney Ridge

Also see:

- **Second-widest diameter cedar street tree in Seattle:** Denny-Blaine, deodar cedar (218 Dorffel Dr. E.)
- **Third- and fifth-widest diameter cedar street trees in Seattle:** Ballard, deodar cedar (7348 26th Ave. NW)
- **Fourth-widest diameter cedar street tree in Seattle:** Magnolia, deodar cedar (1611 28th Ave. W.)
- **First-recorded cedar street tree in the city:** Capitol Hill, Atlas cedar (1405 E. John St.)
- **Widest diameter cedar street trees in District 3:** Leschi, deodar cedar (714 24th Ave. S.)
- **Fourth-widest diameter cedar street tree in District 3:** Capitol Hill, deodar cedar (202 E. 18th Ave.)
- **Second-widest diameter Atlas cedar in District 4:** Wedgwood (7200 28th Ave. NE)
- **Widest diameter cedar of Lebanon street tree in Seattle (out of only 14):** SW Queen Anne (1900 2nd Ave. W.)

other notable street trees :

Almond
(PRUNUS DULCIS)
Max Height : 20'

3-5cm

- small, crooked tree
- white/pale-pink flowers with darker center; fragrant (March)
- 5 petals
- borne singly from branch
- 3" shiny, narrow leaf

notched tip

4 Widest diameter almond street tree in Seattle: 162 NW 62nd St.

Bald Cypress
(TAXODIUM DISTICHUM)
Max Height : 180'

5 Widest diameter bald cypress street tree in Seattle: 713 N. 66th St., a pair

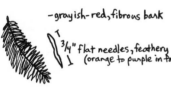

- grayish-red, fibrous bark

3/4" flat needles, feathery (orange to purple in fall)

1" round cone

- twigs alternate on branch (not opposite like Dawn Redwood)

American Basswood Linden **6**
(TILIA AMERICANA)
Max Height : 140'

Third-widest diameter linden street tree in Seattle: 133 N. 50th St.

7" or more heart-shaped leaf; green underneath (not hairy)

yellow flowers in dangling, fragrant clusters (June); become nuts in fall

Black Walnut
(JUGLANS NIGRA)
Max Height: 165'

7 Tied for seventh-widest diameter walnut street tree in Seattle: 203 N. 60th St.

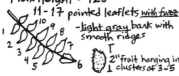

13-27 pointed leaflets

1 2 3 4 5 6 7 8 9 10 11 12

-furrowed bark in diamond pattern, darker than Butternut Walnut

2" round, green nut with grooves (not edible)

Butternut Walnut
(JUGLANS CINEREA)
Max Height: 125'

8 Fifth-widest diameter walnut street tree in Seattle: 6048 1st Ave. NW; listed incorrectly as "English walnut"

11-17 pointed leaflets with fuzz

1 2 3 4 5 6 7 8 9 10

-light gray bark with smooth ridges

2" fruit hanging in clusters of 3-5

European Chestnut
(CASTANEA SATIVA)
Max Height: 120'

9 Widest diameter chestnut street tree in Seattle: 502 N. 47th St., grown into a fire hydrant

In 1904, the famous "chestnut blight" fungus was discovered at today's Bronx Zoo in New York State. It would go on to kill an estimated four billion trees in the United States by the first half of the 20th century. In Seattle, there are 101 chestnut right-of-way trees remaining, mostly European chestnut (the author knows of no American chestnut street trees in the city).

← short stalk

7" leaf with sharp teeth (slightly fuzzy with 14, 18 or 22 veins)
- grayish bark with broad, deep furrows

white flower spikes ♂ (June to July)

3/4" nuts (edible) late-September to early-October

Also see:

- **Second- and fifth-widest diameter chestnut street tree in Seattle:** SW Queen Anne, European chestnut (1314 6th Ave. W.)
- **Fourth-widest diameter chestnut street tree in Seattle (also the first recorded):** Wallingford, European chestnut (1609 N. 49th St.)
- **Sixth-widest diameter chestnut street tree in Seattle:** NW Queen Anne, European chestnut (903 W. Fulton St.)
- **Seventh-widest diameter chestnut street tree in Seattle:** West Seattle (Morgan Junction), European chestnut (5922 41st St. Ave. SW)

Douglas Fir
(PSEUDOTSUGA MENZIESII)
Max Height: 415'

1" soft needle

- deeply furrowed, corky bark

3" cone with bracts sticking out between scales

10 Fifth-widest diameter Douglas fir street tree in Seattle: 6505 Woodland Pl. N.

11 Sixth-widest diameter Douglas fir street tree in Seattle: 503 N. 64th St.

Snow Gum
(EUCALYPTUS PAUCIFLORA)
Max Height: 82'

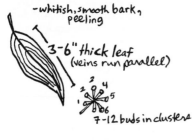

- whitish, smooth bark, peeling

3-6" thick leaf (veins run parallel)

7-12 buds in clusters

12 Tied for eighth-widest eucalyptus street tree in Seattle: 6056 4th Ave. NW (on NW 62nd St.)

Sweet Mazzard Cherry
(PRUNUS AVIUM)

- oval leaf, toothed edges
- white flowers (Mid-April)

bark with horizontal lines

13 Widest mazzard cherry street tree in Seattle: 6216 Evanston Ave. N. (on N. 63rd St.)

European Ash
(FRAXINUS EXCELSIOR)
Max Height: 150'

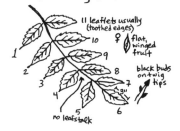

14 Tied as fourth-widest ash street tree in Seattle: 603 N. 49th St.

Pin Oak
(QUERCUS PALUSTRIS)
Max Height: 135'

15 First-recorded oak street trees in Seattle: 5613 Greenwood Ave. N., a pair on N. 57th St. listed on July 9, 1950—the same day a headline on the front page of the *Seattle Daily Times* read "First-to-Go Seattle Draft Men Universally Fatalistic About Call"; the Korean War ended three years later in 1953, and the Korean Peninsula remains divided today

Silk Tree
(ALBIZIA JULIBRISSIN)
Max Height: 60'

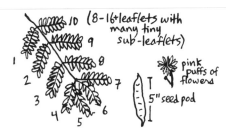

16 Third-widest diameter silk street tree in Seattle: 4903 2nd Ave. NW

Downy birch (*Betula pubescens*)
119 W. Boston St.

Northwest
QUEEN ANNE
Birch

Ten generations of birch can live and die within the life span of a single pine. The birch is short-lived but courageous, often the first tree to colonize barren land. Despite its bravery, it is particularly vulnerable to droughts like the kind the Pacific Northwest has been experiencing in the last decade. In 2016, the *Seattle Times* reported a "treemageddon," with over 500 dead public trees, a 300 percent increase from a typical year. At the University of Washington campus alone, a quarter of the birches had died within two years.

Things had already been looking bleak for the birch: in 2003, the first bronze birch borer was discovered in Portland, a bug that is specifically attracted to the chemicals emitted by dying and distressed birches. "[The birch borers] settle inside the tree and essentially eat away at it for two years and mature before we see any damage, and since birch trees are fairly delicate, by then the damage is irreversible," explained University of Washington arborist Sara Shores in 2018.

Statistics from other cities beset by the birch borer pest suggest we can expect to lose approximately 70 percent of our birch trees. Still, as of 2023, there are roughly 4,300 birch street trees in the city, overall responsible for removing one million pounds of carbon dioxide from our atmosphere each year.

District 7, where Queen Anne is located, has the most paper birch and yellow birch street trees in Seattle.

Birch "the tree of grace"
BETULA
DECIDUOUS
Total: 4,367 (2.5% of all right-of-way trees in Seattle)

W. Fulton St.

11th Ave. W.

⑪

⑨

10th Ave. Pl.

W. Armour St.

⑦

W. Newell St.

W. Bothwell St.

⑤

Mt. Pleasant Cemetery

David Rodgers Park

W. Raye St.

⑬ ⑫ ⑫

⑨

W. Halladay St.

⑥

W. Raye St.

①

W. Smith St.

Westview Dr. W.

10th Ave. W.

9th Ave. W.

8th Ave. W.

7th Ave. W.

W. Wheeler St.

Coe Elementary School

W. McGraw Pl.

W. McGraw Pl.

Queen Anne Ave. W.

W. McGraw St.

⑩

6th Ave. W.

5th Ave. W.

4th Ave. W.

3rd Ave. W.

2nd Ave. W.

1st Ave. W.

W. Boston St.

②

W. Crockett St.

④

W. Crockett St.

McClure Middle School

⑧

W. Howe St.

West Queen Anne Playfield

W. Blaine St.

③

Queen Anne

Also see:

- **Tied for third-widest diameter birch street tree in Seattle:** University District, European birch (5200 16th Ave. NE)
- **Fourth-widest diameter birch street tree in Seattle (also the second-widest paper birch street tree in city):** Ravenna (6278 20th Ave. NE)
- **Seventh-widest diameter birch street tree in Seattle (fourth-widest paper birch in city):** Wallingford (2202 N. 41st St.)

European White Birch
(BETULA PENDULA)
Max Height: 115'

- long stem
- rough white bark with black arrow-shaped furrows
- 3" triangular leaf (double-toothed)
- weeping branches →
- pendent catkins

FROM EUROPE, TURKEY, N. AFRICA

1 Widest diameter European white birch street tree on Queen Anne: 2543 2nd Ave. W.

Downy Birch
(BETULA PUBESCENS)
Max Height: 97'

- downy stalk + twigs
- grayish brown bark (not peeling)
- 2" oval leaf (toothed)
- fluted trunk
- pendent catkins

FROM EUROPE, N. AFRICA

2 Widest diameter birch street tree in Seattle: 119 W. Boston St.; listed as a European white birch

Paper Birch
(BETULA PAPYRIFERA)
Max Height: 120'

- white bark peeling at edges
- 3½" oval leaf (double-toothed); 5-10 pairs of veins
- pendent catkins

FROM ALASKA, CANADA, NORTHERN UNITED STATES

3 Widest diameter paper birch street tree in Seattle (tied for third-widest birch street tree in Seattle overall): 321 W. Blaine St.

Whitebarked Himalayan Birch
(BETULA UTILIS VAR. JACQUEMONTII)
Max Height: 79'

- often red stalk
- shiny white to pinkish bark, peeling
- 3" glossy leaf; 7-9 pairs of veins
- pendent catkins

FROM W. HIMALAYAS

4 Widest diameter whitebarked Himalayan birch street tree in District 7: 1958 5th Ave. W. (on W. Crockett St.)

Yellow Birch
(BETULA ALLEGHANIENSIS)
Max Height: 100'

- short stalk
- yellowish bronze bark, sometimes peeling or in plates
- 4" oval leaf (double-toothed); 12-15 pairs of veins
- shaggy, upright catkins

FROM EASTERN N. AMERICA

5 Fifth-widest diameter birch street tree in Seattle (also widest yellow birch street tree in city): 2661 8th Ave. W.

QUEEN ANNE (Northwest)
other notable street trees :

Bigleaf Linden
(TILIA PLATYPHYLLOS)

6 First-recorded linden street tree in Seattle: 520 W. Raye St., in front of building; surrounded by Crimean lindens, listed on August 19, 1959

Bigleaf Maple
(ACER MACROPHYLLUM)

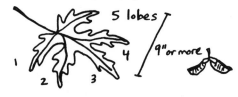

7 Tied for sixth-widest diameter maple street tree in Seattle: 2707 9th Ave. W. (on W. Newell St.)

Cedar of Lebanon
(CEDRUS LIBANI)

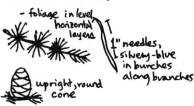

8 Widest diameter cedar of Lebanon street tree in Seattle (out of only 14): 1900 2nd Ave. W., bordering west side of McClure School; listed incorrectly as "deodar cedar"

European Chestnut
(CASTANEA SATIVA)

9 Sixth-widest diameter chestnut street tree in Seattle: 903 W. Fulton St.

Ginkgo
(GINKGO BILOBA)

🔟 Third-widest diameter ginkgo street tree in Seattle: 2558 9th Ave. W.

fan shaped leaf, variable shapes

1" orange fruit (late Sep-Oct)

knobby twigs

Norway Spruce
(PICEA ABIES)

⑪ Second-widest diameter spruce street tree in Seattle: 1007 W. Fulton St.

3/4" rigid needles

-drooping twigs

4.9" cone with jagged-tipped scales

Pin Oak
(QUERCUS PALUSTRIS)

⑫ Widest- and second-widest diameter pin oak street trees in Seattle: 2560 and 2575 10th Ave. W.

-narrow upright trunk

5 1/2 deeply-lobed leaf

-smooth bark

5/8" tiny acorns

Western Red Cedar
(THUJA PLICATA)

⑬ Tied for fifth-widest diameter Western red cedar street tree in Seattle: 1007 Raye St., three-trunked specimen

-reddish, fibrous bark; often fluted and buttressed

lacy scale-like foliage

1/3" upright cone

European beech (*Fagus sylvatica*)
202 W. Prospect St. on 2nd Ave. W

southwest
QUEEN ANNE
Beech

The beech is rarely seen as a street tree due to its giant size, and is more commonly seen in parks, cemeteries, and golf courses, but Seattle still has a healthy 1,009 beech right-of-way trees to call its own. The widest diameter beech in the City of Seattle's data is a copper beech at Volunteer Park included because it is a Heritage Tree, a designation of both public and private trees that can be nominated by anyone. (Contrary to popular belief, there is no legal protection for these trees.)

The elephant-like trunk of the beech is a surface that has been inviting human graffiti and carvings since the dawn of civilization. Like human skin, once the beech passes "middle age," its bark begins to wrinkle. Another way to tell the age of a beech is to observe where the foliage begins growing: the older the tree, the farther up the trunk it begins branching out. Also notable, unlike most deciduous trees, the beech's leaves are "marcescent" (some oaks are as well), meaning they don't shed in fall; instead, they turn brown but remain on the branches into winter (it is nearly impossible to tell a copper beech from a common European beech in autumn). As seasons change in Seattle and days grow longer and shorter, the beech is able to adapt, withholding new leaves only until it is light for at least 13 hours a day.

District 7, which includes southwest Queen Anne, has the largest concentration of the widest diameter beech street trees in the city. In the late 1800s, Queen Anne was also known as Eden Hill, Galer Hill, and—hilariously—North Seattle.

"the tree of prosperity"

Beech

FAGUS
DECIDUOUS
Total: 1,009 (0.6% of all right-of-way trees in Seattle)

Copper Beech
(Fagus sylvatica f purpurea)
Max Height: 100'

FROM EUROPE, W. ASIA

1 Tied as city's second-widest diameter beech tree (when including trees in the right-of-way): 1400 8th Ave. W., corner of yard

2 W. Galer St. between 7th and 8th Ave. W.: 1432 8th Ave. W., midway up stairway, bordering yard; not included in the city's data

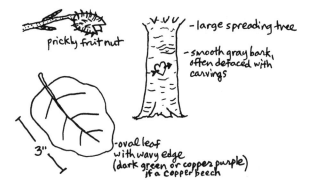

prickly fruit nut

– large spreading tree

– smooth gray bark, often defaced with carvings

– oval leaf with wavy edge (dark green or copper purple) if a copper beech

3"

European Beech
(Fagus sylvatica)
Max Height: 164'

FROM EUROPE, W. ASIA

3 Tied as city's second-widest diameter beech tree (when including trees in the right-of-way): 200 W. Blaine St., bordering West Queen Anne Playfield, recorded in 1975

4 Third-widest diameter beech street tree in Seattle: 1522 3rd Ave. W.

5 Eighth-widest diameter beech street tree in Seattle (when including trees in the right-of-way): 202 W. Prospect St., on 2nd Ave. W., bordering yard at bottom of stairs just below Kerry Park

southwest
Queen Anne

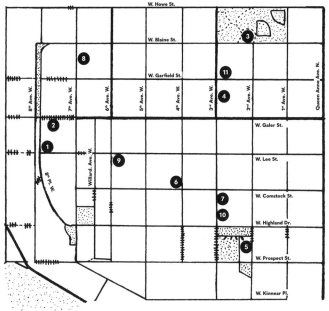

Also see:

- **Widest diameter beech street tree in Seattle (when including Heritage Trees in public parks):** Capitol Hill at Volunteer Park, copper beech (1400 E. Prospect St.)
- **Widest diameter beech street tree in Seattle in a parking strip:** Madison Valley, European beech (1733 39th Ave.)
- **Second-widest diameter beech street tree in Seattle:** Cherry Hill, European beech (815 18th Ave.)
- **Fourth- and fifth-widest diameter beech street trees in Seattle:** Capitol Hill, European beech (510 17th Ave. E.)
- **First-recorded beech street trees in Seattle:** Beacon Hill, European beech (3014 and 3020 Beacon Ave. S.)
- **Other notable specimens not in data:** Lake View Cemetery, copper and European beech, Capitol Hill (1554 15th Ave. E.)

Copper beech (*Fagus sylvatica purpurea*)
1400 8th Ave. W.

American elm (*Ulmus americana*)
402 Comstock St. on 4th Ave. W.

QUEEN ANNE (Southwest)
other notable street trees:

American Elm
(ULMUS AMERICANA)

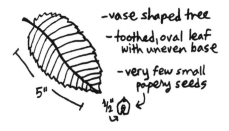

-vase shaped tree

-toothed, oval leaf
  with uneven base

-very few small
  papery seeds

5"

½" (e)

6 Widest diameter elm street tree in
Seattle: 402 Comstock St.; on 4th Ave.
W., listed incorrectly as "Chinese elm"

Bigleaf Maple
(ACER MACROPHYLLUM)

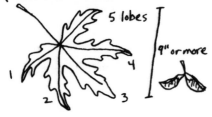

5 lobes

9" or more

1 2 3 4

7 Tied as third-widest diameter maple street tree in Seattle: 1224 3rd Ave. W.

Black Walnut
(JUGLANS NIGRA)

13-27 pointed leaflets (toothed)

-dark, furrowed bark

2" nut

8 Second-widest diameter walnut street tree in Seattle: 1620 7th Ave. W.

European chestnut
(CASTANEA SATIVA)

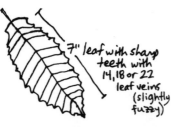

7" leaf with sharp teeth with 14, 18 or 22 leaf veins (slightly fuzzy)

spiky nut husks (ripe mid-September to early-October)

5"

♂ spikes of white male flowers (June to July)

9 Second- and fifth-widest diameter chestnut street trees in Seattle: 1314 6th Ave. W., on W. Lee St.

Lombardy Poplar
(POPULUS NIGRA 'ITALICA')

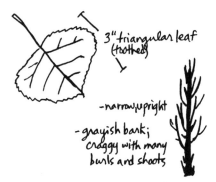

3" triangular leaf (toothed)

-narrow, upright

- grayish bark; craggy with many burls and shoots

10 Second-widest diameter poplar street tree in Seattle: 222 Highland Dr., on 3rd Ave. W.

Norway Spruce
(PICEA ABIES)

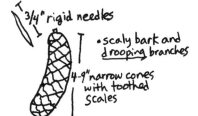

3/4" rigid needles

• scaly bark and drooping branches

4-9" narrow cones with toothed scales

11 Third-widest diameter spruce street tree in the city: 1602 3rd Ave. W., on W. Garfield St., listed incorrectly as "white spruce"

12 Widest diameter dawn redwood street trees in Seattle: 1820 Warren Ave. N.

RAVENNA Hemlock

Early loggers believed hemlock to be commercially inferior "weed" trees, leaving them relatively untouched. It wasn't until after World War I that new chemical methods rendered the trees good for making "green gold" (a.k.a. pulp for things like newsprint).

Due to its new importance, in 1946 the Western hemlock was suggested by the *Portland Oregonian* to be Washington state's official tree. The *Wenatchee World* disagreed, suggesting the apple instead and, as if in punishment, due to a newsprint shortage later that year, the staff was forced to log four carloads of hemlock on their own so they could continue printing the news. From another part of the state, the *Longview News* nominated the Western Red Cedar and the *Seattle Daily Times* joined them in declaring, "Down with the Hemlock; let the Red Cedar reign supreme." What the *Seattle Daily Times* called "the furor over the State of Washington's embarrassing lack of an official tree" continued when Joseph R. Hillaire of the Suquamish wrote a letter to the editor on behalf of the Native Americans of the state, joining in the preference for Western Red Cedar.

Despite the clear public preference, in 1947 the western hemlock became the official tree for the state of Washington anyway. Three years later, Washington's paper manufacturing eclipsed its lumber production.

District 4, which includes Ravenna, is home to the widest diameter hemlock street tree in the city (which isn't really that wide).

Western hemlock (*Tsuga heterophylla*)
7558 Brooklyn Ave. NE

Hemlock "the tree of longevity"

TSUGA
EVERGREEN
Total: 447 (0.2% of all right-of-way trees in Seattle)

NE. 77th St.

NE. 75th St.

NE. 75th St.

Roosevelt Reservoir

NE. 73rd St.

NE. 73rd St.

NE. 72nd St.

NE. 71st St.

NE. 70th St.

NE. 70th St.

NE. 69th St.

NE. 68th St.

NE. 68th St.

NE. 67th St.

Roosevelt High School

Ravenna Eckstein Park

NE. 66th St.

16th Ave. NE.

17th Ave. NE.

18th Ave. NE.

19th Ave. NE.

20th Ave. NE.

21st Ave. NE.

22nd Ave. NE.

Ravenna Ave. NE.

NE. 65th St.

8th Ave. NE.

9th Ave. NE.

Roosevelt Ave. NE.

12th Ave. NE.

Brooklyn Ave. NE.

14th Ave. NE.

15th Ave. NE.

NE. 64th St.

NE. 63rd St.

Whitman Park

NE. Naomi Pl.

NE. 62nd St.

Ravenna Park

Eastern Hemlock
(TSUGA CANADENSIS)
Max Height: 176'

½" flat, blunt-tipped needle

½" cone

needles strongly 2-ranked on branch, flat

FROM EASTERN N. AMERICA

 6601 Roosevelt Way NE, on NE 66th St.

180

Western Hemlock
(TSUGA HETEROPHYLLA)
Max Height: 259'

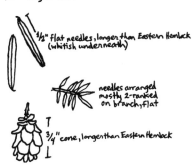

½" flat needles, longer than Eastern Hemlock (whitish underneath)

needles arranged mostly 2-ranked on branch, flat

¾" cone, longer than Eastern Hemlock

NATIVE FROM S. ALASKA
TO N. CALIFORNIA

② **Widest diameter hemlock street tree in Seattle:** 7558 Brooklyn Ave. NE, on NE 77th St., east of a Douglas fir on the corner

③ **Second-widest diameter hemlock street tree in Seattle:** 6902 12th Ave. NE, on NE 69th St.

A Deeper Dig

Ravenna was best known in the early 20th century for the large trees in the ravine today known as Ravenna Park. The widest diameter Ravenna Douglas fir was named after then-president Theodore "Teddy" Roosevelt (an avowed conservationist who personally visited his namesake tree). Then, to everyone's horror, in 1913 the Seattle Federation of Women's Clubs discovered that the Roosevelt tree had been cut down by the city park superintendent, who defended himself by claiming the tree was a "threat to public safety." He shamelessly added that the tree had produced 63 cords of wood that he'd sold to help pay for the cost of its removal. Park historian Don Sherwood said in a 1972 interview with the *Seattle Post-Intelligencer*, "It was common practice in those days to call a healthy tree diseased and cut it down."

In 1920, a year after the human Roosevelt died and Roosevelt Way and Roosevelt High School were named in his honor, the superintendent was pressured to resign due to "abuse of office and intoxication." (Still, the Seattle Parks Department went on in 1926 to chop down the last of the old growth giants in the Ravenna ravine.)

RAVENNA
other notable street trees:

Bigleaf Maple
(ACER MACROPHYLLUM)

5 lobes

9" or more

4 Fourth-widest diameter maple street tree in the city: 1201 NE 69th St.

Common Orchard Apple
(MALUS X DOMESTICA)

- spreading tree; tangled branches

3" toothed leaf

5"+

1¼" pink flowers (March to April)

5 Second-widest diameter common orchard apple street tree in Seattle: 7534 21st Ave. NE

Douglas Fir
(PSEUDOTSUGA MENZIESII)

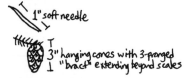
1" soft needle

3" hanging cones with 3-pronged "bract" extending beyond scales

6 Third-widest diameter Douglas fir street tree in Seattle: 6818 19th Ave. NE

English Walnut
(JUGLANS REGIA)

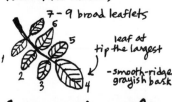
7 - 9 broad leaflets

leaf at tip the largest

- smooth-ridged grayish bark

2½" nut (September)

7 Third-widest diameter English walnut street tree in Seattle: 6524 16th Ave. NE

Saucer Magnolia
(MAGNOLIA X SOULANGEANA)
Max Height: 51'

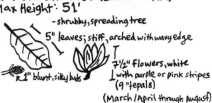
- shrubby, spreading tree

5" leaves; stiff, arched with wavy edge

1" blunt, silky buds

7½" flowers, white with purple or pink stripes (9 "tepals) (March/April through August)

8 Tied as sixth-widest diameter magnolia street tree in Seattle: 1308 NE 62nd St.

Common orchard apple (*Malus × domestica*)
7534 21st Ave. NE

Italian Cypress
(CUPRESSUS SEMPERVIRENS)
Max Height: 164'

9 Widest diameter true cypress street tree in Seattle: 7051 Ravenna Ave. NE

scaly foliage radiating in all directions from branch

-rough, fibrous bark

-wide-spreading in natural form, or "flame-shaped" if pruned

1 1/3" round "cone"

Norway Spruce
(PICEA ABIES)

10 Third-widest diameter spruce street tree in Seattle: 1253 NE 69th St.

-scaly gray bark with drooping branches

3/4" rigid needles

4-9"cone, narrow with slightly toothed scales

Paper Birch
(BETULA PAPYRIFERA)

11 Second-widest paper birch street tree in city: 6278 20th Ave. NE

short stalk

- peeling white bark

3 1/2" toothed leaf

fruiting catkins

Peach
(PRUNUS PERSICA)

(non-fruiting cultivar)
6-8" long, narrow, drooping leaf (toothed)

fuzzy buds

2 ⚘ 5 pink flowers (March - April)
3 4

12 Possibly the oldest miniature street tree in the city: 6533 20th Ave. NE, next to fire hydrant, is a "dwarf" tree listed only as "peach" on July 29, 2009, but actually replaced one planted in 1969

Southern Catalpa
(CATALPA BIGNONIOIDES)

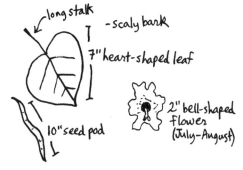

long stalk
- scaly bark
7" heart-shaped leaf
10" seed pod
2" bell-shaped flower (July-August)

13 Ninth-widest diameter catalpa street tree in Seattle: 6311 17th Ave. NE

Yoshino Cherry
(PRUNUS x YEDOENSIS)

5 petals
· pink flowers (late-March)
· bark with horizontal lines

14 Tied for third-widest diameter cherry street trees in city: 1315 NE 70th St.

ROANOKE
Elm

In the early 20th century, University of Washington professor Edmund J. Meany planted an elm scion on the campus grounds sent to him by a former student who was studying at Harvard. The student had gathered the shoots from the famous Washington Elm of Cambridge, Massachusetts, under which legend has it that George Washington took command of the Continental Army on July 3, 1775. When the original tree in Cambridge fell over in 1923 after more than 200 years, cuttings of the one grown in Seattle were sent back so that clones of the storied elm could grow all over again.

The 1930s were a bleak time for both America and the elm: The same year as the great Black Monday stock market crash of 1929, the first cases of Dutch elm disease, or DED, were discovered in the United States, wiping out elms in the east and midwest where they represented as high as 75 percent of planted trees. The clone of the Washington elm at UW appeared safe for many decades, until it was struck by lightning in 1963. (This time, it was Cambridge that sent Seattle saplings grown from the tree it had raised from the UW elm cuttings.)

DED was not detected in the state of Washington until the 1970s and the effects were not visible in Seattle until 2001. The clone of the clone of the clone of the Washington Elm at UW is no longer there, having cracked in 2016—but a clone of the clone lives on at the Washington Park Arboretum.

The neighborhood of Roanoke is home to a group of 25 mature elms in and around Roanoke Park, which were planted in 1910.

English elm (*Ulmus procera*)
1 Broadway Ave. E.

Elm "the tree of dignity"
ULMUS
DECIDUOUS
Total: 2,627 (1.5% of all right-of-way trees in Seattle)

American Elm
(ULMUS AMERICANA)
Max Height: 160'

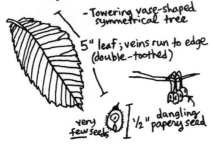

- Towering vase-shaped symmetrical tree
- 5" leaf; veins run to edge (double-toothed)
- very few seeds
- ½" dangling papery seed

FROM CENTRAL AND EASTERN UNITED STATES

① 815 E. Edgar St., in front of church, two flanking one European white elm

English Elm
(ULMUS MINOR)
Max Height: 165'

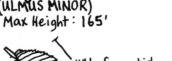

- 4" leaf, roundish and often crumpled (double-toothed)
- 1"
- "corky" grooved twigs

FROM ENGLAND, EUROPE

② 1 Broadway Ave. E., street trees bordering north side of park

European White Elm
(ULMUS LAEVIS)
Max Height: 160'

- trunk with lots of sprouts
- 5" leaf; up to 19 pairs of veins, rarely branching (double-toothed)
- very uneven base
- leaf broadest beyond midpoint
- ½" seed like American Elm but rounder, with many more produced

FROM CENTRAL AND SE EUROPE, W. ASIA

③ 815 E. Edgar St., between two American elms in front of church

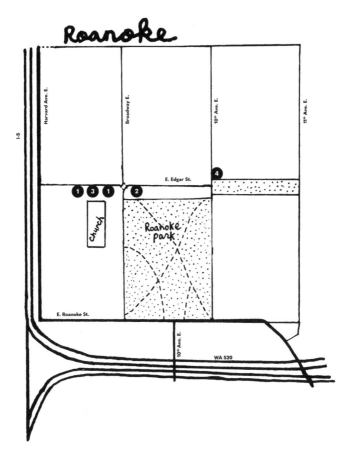

Roanoke

Also see:

- **Widest diameter elm street tree in Seattle:** Queen Anne, American elm (402 Comstock St.)
- **Second-widest and tied for sixth-widest diameter elm street trees in Seattle:** West Seattle (Admiral), English elms (1439 Sunset Ave. SW)
- **Third-widest diameter elm street tree in Seattle:** University District, American elm (1507 NE Ravenna Blvd.)
- **Tied as eighth-widest diameter elm street tree:** Capitol Hill, American elm (1110 E. John St.). *Not illustrated:* English elm (611 13th Ave. E.); Washington Park, English elms (1039 36th Ave. E.)
- **Tied as ninth-widest diameter elm street tree:** West Seattle (Admiral), American elm (1934 42nd Ave. SW); Madison Park, English elms (1039 and 1101 36th Ave. E.)
- **First-recorded elm street tree in Seattle:** *Not illustrated:* Capitol Hill, Guernsey elm *(Ulmus minor 'Sarniensis')* (807 E. Roy St.), NW corner of old Woman's Century Club (likely planted when built in 1925)
- **Mount Baker's second-widest diameter street tree:** American elm (2827 33rd Ave. S.)

ROANOKE
other notable street tree:

Common Horse Chestnut ❹
(AESCULUS HIPPOCASTANUM)

Widest diameter street tree in Roanoke and the fifth-widest horse chestnut street tree in District 3: 2700 10th Ave. E.

–white flowers in clusters; yellow and red markings (May bloom)

14" leaf with 7 leaflets

Everything Is Connected

Forest ecologist Suzanne Simard was the first to discover that forest trees communicate with each other, sharing nutrients and information via fungal networks that connect with a tree's roots and extend its reach. Her research has shown how resources are shared among different trees, using dye to visually demonstrate how hundreds of pounds of carbon are moved between species through their underground "mycorrhizal" associations (fungal roots that form symbiotic relationships with trees).

Simard calls this phenomenon the "Wood Wide Web," likening the fungal connections to fiber-optic internet cables that transmit electrical signals. Mostly invisible to the naked eye, fungi make up nearly half of all soil globally, and a single teaspoon of forest soil can contain miles of fungal threads, with one fungus in Oregon estimated to extend 2,000 acres. Long before humans created the internet, the most complex and sophisticated networks were already functioning.

Street trees, of course, are more limited than their forest counterparts. One study conducted by ecological engineer Nadina Galle revealed that the soil of red maple street trees in Boston, Massachusetts, had low mycorrhizal fungi colonization, suggesting they have trouble engaging with their tree neighbors. Typically planted in isolated pits in rows that keep them apart, street trees live relatively "lonely" lives devoid of the shared resources their community might otherwise supply.

With recent droughts, heat waves, and changing climate, the stress faced by solitary street trees manifests as vulnerability to diseases that did not previously affect them. As it turns out, everything actually is connected, loneliness can kill, and survival is directly dependent on the strength of one's network.

Southern catalpa (*Catalpa bignonioides*)
1218 S. Sullivan St.

SOUTH PARK *Catalpa*

In 1930, near the beginning of the Great Depression, the South Park Boosters Club set out to plant specific trees in parking strips on certain streets, including "mop head catalpa on Donovan Street." The event made Seattle history as the "first time in the city that a concentrated effort [had] been made to plant entire districts upon a system worked out by arboriculturists." Up until this point, street trees in Seattle had been planted haphazardly, with no coordination, despite statements like one in the *Seattle Daily Times* in 1911 contending that "the mixing of kinds of trees in a single block brings most inartistic results."

The trend of planting single trees on a street would, however, be controversial. During World War II, in 1942, members of the Seattle City Council toured the same catalpa-lined streets in South Park in order to witness for themselves "an exhibit of proper planting with attractive results." This act prompted the *Seattle Daily Times* to state that "an occasional catalpa, here and there, may look very well in full summer foliage . . . but the bare suggestion that *bignoniaceous* uniformity would be a 'proper planting' of all parking strips in the city, sends shudders through the membership of every improvement and community club." (Of course, the uniform planting of street trees became commonplace in the 1970s.)

There are only 338 catalpa right-of-way trees in all of Seattle, and District 1, where South Park is located, has the most as well as some of the oldest.

"the tree of caution"
CATALPA
DECIDUOUS
Total: 338 (0.2% of all right-of-way trees in Seattle)

Northern Catalpa
(CATALPA SPECIOSA)
Max Height: 150'

← long stalk

- flowers in clusters (late-June to early July)

8" heart-shaped leaf, some with lobes

- contorted branches; twisted trunk

14" seed pod (remains through winter)

FROM CENTRAL UNITED STATES

1 Center traffic island at intersection of 10th Ave. S. and S. Rose St.; baby street tree planted in 2021

Southern Catalpa
(CATALPA BIGNONIOIDES)
Max Height: 90'

← long stalk

- scaly bark

7" heart-shaped leaf (rarely lobed)

dwarf cultivar leaves smaller, slightly hairy

10" seed pod (remains through winter)

2" bell-shaped flowers; white with purple and yellow markings (July-August)

(dwarf cultivar is flowerless)

FROM SOUTHERN UNITED STATES

2 **Fifth-widest diameter catalpa street tree in Seattle:** 1218 S. Sullivan St., a tree that has reverted to its original, tall southern catalpa form; this street is otherwise lined with a *flowerless* dwarf cultivar called umbrella catalpa (*Catalpa bignonioides* 'Nana')

3 **First-recorded catalpa street trees in Seattle:** Widest at 8700 10th Ave., a dwarf that has reverted to its natural, large tree form; others here listed in city's data on January 1, 1963, but likely much older

South Park

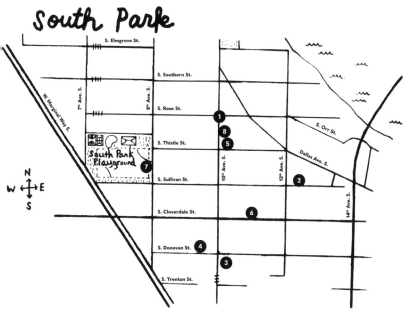

Also see:

- **Widest diameter catalpa street tree in Seattle:** Cherry Hill, northern catalpa (1124 19th Ave.)
- **Second-widest diameter catalpa street tree in Seattle:** Wallingford, southern catalpa (3614 Bagley Ae. N.)
- **Eighth-widest diameter catalpa street tree in Seattle:** Green Lake, southern catalpa (6540 1st Ave. NE)
- **Ninth-widest diameter catalpa street tree in Seattle:** Ravenna, southern catalpa (6311 17th Ave. NE)
- **Tied for 10th-widest diameter catalpa street tree in Seattle:** Columbia City, southern catalpa (4702 S. Ferdinand St.); *Not illustrated:* East Capitol Hill, Southern catalpa (1741 Belmont Ave.)
- **Mount Baker's widest diameter catalpa street trees:** Southern (umbrella) catalpa (3210 S. Lander St.)

SOUTH PARK
other notable street trees:

Chitalpa
(CHITALPA TASHKENTENSIS)

6" narrow, pointed leaf

pink and white flowers in clusters (July-August)

④ Seattle's "lost" chitalpa street tree: 838 S. Donovan St., not included in the city's data is this early 1960s hybrid related to the southern catalpa and created in Uzbekistan; planted in Seattle since the 1990s, unlike catalpa, its pink or white clusters of flowers bloom all summer

Coast Redwood
(SEQUOIA SEMPERVIRENS)

1" feathery needles in flat sprays

- reddish, fibrous bark

1" cone

⑤ Sixth-widest diameter coast redwood street tree in Seattle (when including trees in the right-of-way): 8320 10th Ave. S.; listed on January 1, 1965, the same month the Beach Boys played at the Seattle Coliseum (which was converted into a Banana Republic clothing store in 1994 and is a temporary art space in 2023)

Ginkgo
(GINKGO BILOBA)

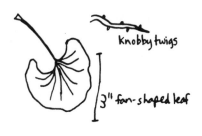

knobby twigs

3" fan-shaped leaf

⑥ First-recorded and widest diameter ginkgo tree in data set (when including right-of-way trees): 1032 S. Cloverdale St., male tree hanging over the sidewalk; listed on December 31, 1950, one month before Seattle would experience its coldest temperature ever recorded, 0 degrees Fahrenheit (the city has not been colder than 10 degrees Fahrenheit since 1989)

Lombardy Poplar
(POPULUS NIGRA 'ITALICA')

7 **8th Ave. S., north of S. Sullivan St.:** a giant at 738 S. Sullivan St., east border of South Park Playground; not in city's data

3″

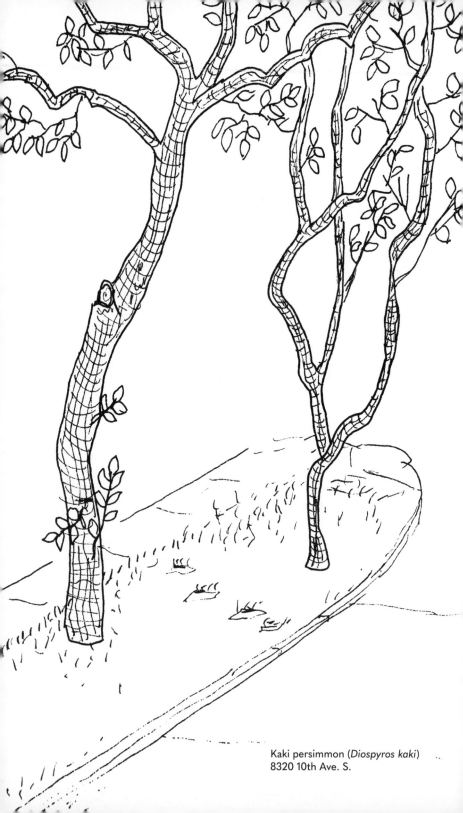

Kaki persimmon (*Diospyros kaki*)
8320 10th Ave. S.

DIOSPYROS
DECIDUOUS
Total: 60 (0.03% of all right-of-way trees in Seattle)

Kaki Persimmon
(Diospyros kaki)
Max Height: 60'

(8) First-recorded and third-widest diameter persimmon street trees in Seattle: 8320 10th Ave. S., three incorrectly listed in the city's data as "American persimmon" on January 1, 1975, the same day President Richard M. Nixon's former US attorney general and chief of staff were convicted of conspiracy, obstruction of justice, and perjury in the cover-up of the Watergate scandal

7" leaf with pointed tip

2½" orange fruit

American Persimmon
(DIOSPYROS VIRGINIANA)
Max Height: 131'

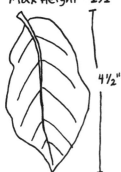

4½"

- pointed oval leaf with wavy edge
- orange fruit (remaining through winter)
- crooked trunk, contorted branches (bark broken into checkers)

1'½" orange fruit

(ripe late October to February)

tiny white flowers (late June)

Also see:

- **Widest and second-widest diameter persimmon street trees in Seattle:** Wallingford, American persimmon (1408 N. 47th St.)
- **Seventh-widest diameter persimmon street trees in Seattle:** Bryant, American persimmon (4501 NE 60th St.)

Common horse chestnut (*Aesculus hippocastanum*)
4503 17th Ave. NE

UNIVERSITY DISTRICT
Horse Chestnut

In 1895, the University of Washington relocated from present-day downtown Seattle to its current location in the University District (formerly known as Brooklyn), and—thanks to the Olmsted Brothers' "Plan for Parks and Boulevards" submitted to the City of Seattle in 1903—a new horse chestnut–lined "University Boulevard" was established on 17th Avenue NE, a rolling parkway leading to the university entrance and extending north to Ravenna Boulevard. Native forests were cleared from the land in 1906, and the showpiece promenade was paved and planted with its original horse chestnut street trees in 1909 in preparation for the Alaska-Yukon-Pacific Exposition, held that year on the UW campus.

Horse chestnuts (poisonous and not to be confused with edible chestnuts) were introduced to Western gardens from the eastern Mediterranean in the 17th century, and first became popular street trees in the 18th century. In the mid-1800s, French emperor Napoléon III famously replaced the elms lining the Champs-Élysées in Paris with horse chestnuts. They were prized for their grand size, shade, and showy flower clusters, commonly used in public parks, golf courses, and university grounds that had large lawns. Although not native to the Pacific Northwest, horse chestnuts are now naturalizing in Seattle, meaning they have adapted to their new home so well that they are able to reproduce and spread on their own.

Today, there are roughly 1,155 horse-chestnut right-of-way trees in Seattle, and District 4, which includes the University District, has the most. The University of Washington is one of the oldest universities on the West Coast.

Horse Chestnut

"the tree of good luck"
AESCULUS
DECIDUOUS
Total: 1,155 (0.7% of all right-of-way trees in Seattle)

Common Horse Chestnut
(AESCULUS HIPPOCASTANUM)
Max Height: 134'

- ~14" leaf, 7 leaflets
- thick, upswept twigs; sticky buds
- white flowers in 10" clusters; yellow markings turn red after pollination (May bloom)
- 2" spiny fruit with shiny nuts in fall

├── 14" ──┤   10"

FROM GREECE, ALBANIA

❶ **Fourth-widest diameter horse chestnut street tree in Seattle:** 17th Ave. NE between NE 45th St. and Ravenna Blvd.: lining street, with widest at 4503 17th Ave. NE; listed incorrectly in the city's data as a "redflower horse chestnut"

Redflower Horse Chestnut
(AESCULUS X CARNEA)
Max Height: 90'

- 8" leaf, 5 leaflets (sometimes 7)
- less prickly nut husk than Common Horse Chestnut

8"

 VS.

- reddish flowers (May)

6"

HYBRIDIZED IN EUROPE, 1800s

❷ NE 17th St. north of NE 50th St.: center median, two very young trees

Yellow Buckeye
(AESCULUS FLAVA)
Max Height: 152'

- 9" leaf, 5-7 leaflets (pointed)
- Fall color brighter and earlier than Common Horse chestnut
- yellow flowers (May)
- smooth nut husk

├── 9" ──┤   6"

FROM EASTERN UNITED STATES

❸ NE Ravenna Blvd. east of 21st Ave. NE: center median, several among common horse chestnut

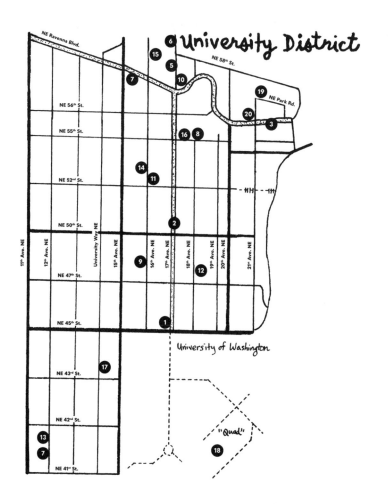

University District

Also see:

- **Tied as widest diameter horse chestnut in Seattle:** *Not illustrated:* Ballard (1007 NW 67th St.) and Madison Valley (1016 32nd Ave. E.)
- **Second-widest diameter horse chestnut in Seattle:** Capitol Hill (1151 19th Ave. E.)

other notable street trees:

American White Elm
(ULMUS AMERICANA)

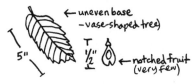
← uneven base
– vase-shaped tree)
5"
T ½"
← notched fruit
(very few)

4 Third-widest diameter elm street tree in Seattle: 1507 NE Ravenna Blvd.

Bigleaf Maple
(ACER MACROPHYLLUM)

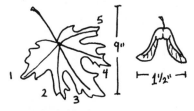
5
9"
4
1
2
3
⊢ 1½" ⊣

5 Tied as widest diameter maple street tree in Seattle: 5723 17th Ave. NE

Black Locust
(ROBINIA PSEUDOACACIA)

7–20 leaflets
– rugged, furrowed bark with zig-zag branches, double-thorns
1½"
hanging clusters of white, fragrant flowers (May–June)

6 Tied for sixth-widest diameter black locust street tree in Seattle: 5813 17th Ave. NE

Chinese Scholar Tree
(SOPHORA JAPONICA)

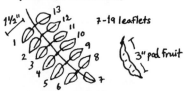
1½"
13
12
11
10
9
8
7-19 leaflets
1
2
3
4
5
6
7
3" pod fruit

7 Widest diameter Chinese scholar street tree in Seattle: 4115 12th Ave. NE, south of widest plane street tree in the city, incorrectly recorded as black locust

English Holly
(ILEX AQUIFOLIUM)

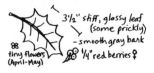
3½" stiff, glossy leaf (some prickly)
– smooth gray bark
tiny flowers (April-May)
¼" red berries ♀

8 Tied as widest diameter and second-widest English holly street trees in Seattle: 1802 NE 55th St., a female pair

Austrian Pine
(PINUS NIGRA)

9 Widest diameter Austrian pine street tree in Seattle: 4715 16th Ave. NE

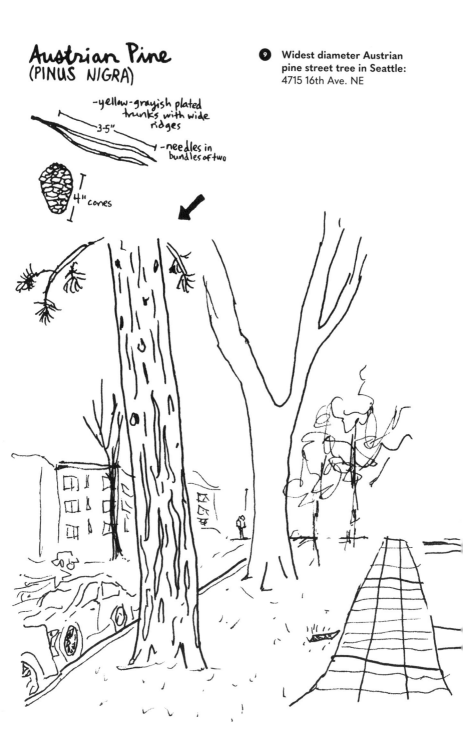

-yellow-grayish plated trunks with wide ridges

3-5"

-needles in bundles of two

4" cones

English Walnut
(JUGLANS REGIA)

7-9 leaflets

- smooth-ridged gray bark

2½" glossy nut (Mid-September)

10 Second-widest diameter English walnut street tree in Seattle: 5706 17th Ave. NE

European White Birch
(BETULA PENDULA)

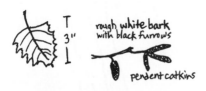

3"

rough white bark with black furrows

pendent catkins

11 Tied for third-widest birch street tree in Seattle: 5200 16th Ave. NE

Lawson Cypress
(CHAMAECYPARIS LAWSONIA)

- fibrous reddish bark
- scaly foliage, fan-shaped spray

⅜" seed cone

12 Fourth-widest diameter false cypress street tree in Seattle: 4722 18th Ave. NE

London Plane
(PLATANUS X ACERIFOLIA)

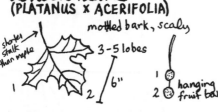

mottled bark, scaly

shorter stalk than maple

3-5 lobes

6"

hanging fruit balls

13 Seattle's widest diameter London plane street tree: 4123 12th Ave. NE, north of city's widest Chinese scholar street tree

Pacific Dogwood
(CORNUS NUTTALLII)

- leaf veins curving parallel to edge

6 white petals (mid-April bloom)

5½"

14 Second-widest diameter dogwood street tree in Seattle: 5225 16th Ave. NE

Pin Oak
(QUERCUS PALUSTRIS)

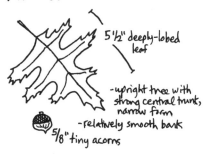

5½" deeply-lobed leaf

-upright tree with strong central trunk, narrow form
-relatively smooth bark
⅝" tiny acorns

15 Tied as seventh-widest diameter oak street tree in Seattle: 5806 16th Ave. NE

Sawara Cypress
(CHAMAECYPARIS PISIFERA)
Max Height: 164'

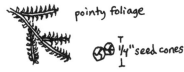

pointy foliage

¼" seed cones

16 Sixth-widest diameter false cypress street tree in Seattle and widest sawara cypress: 1724 NE 55th St.

'Shirotae' Flowering Cherry
(PRUNUS 'SHIROTAE')
Max Height: 33'

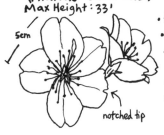

5cm

- flat-topped tree
- long-fringed leaves
- White flowers; fragrant (early April)
- 5-11 petals
- flowers in clusters of 4-6

notched tip

17 University District's only 'Shirotae' cherry street tree: 4306 University Way NE, in front of Shiga's Imports, mistakenly recorded in city's data on April Fool's Day as Columnar Sargent cherry; Shiga's opened in 1956 and helped launch the University District Street Fair in 1970, now the country's longest-running street fair

Yoshino Cherry
(PRUNUS X YEDOENSIS)

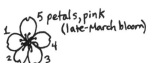

5 petals, pink (late-March bloom)

18 University of Washington Quad: beloved old Yoshino trees transplanted here in 1962 from their original location at the Arboretum, where they were planted in 1936 before Interstate 520 was constructed

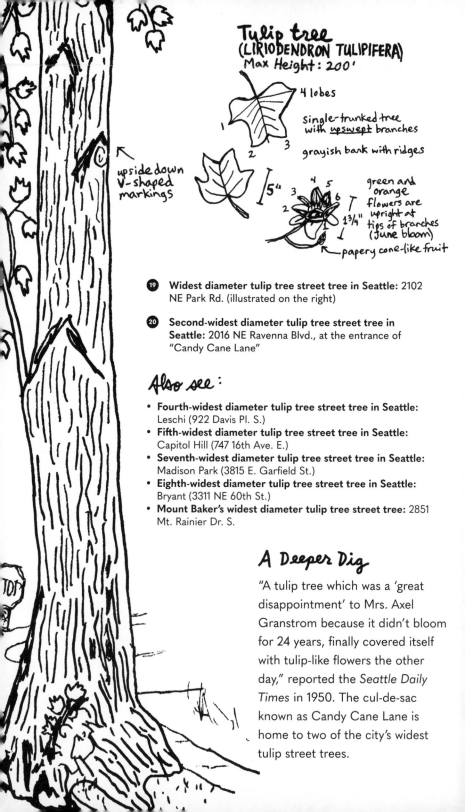

Tulip tree
(LIRIODENDRON TULIPIFERA)
Max Height: 200'

4 lobes

single-trunked tree with _upswept_ branches

grayish bark with ridges

upside down V-shaped markings

green and orange flowers are upright at tips of branches (June bloom)

papery cone-like fruit

19 Widest diameter tulip tree street tree in Seattle: 2102 NE Park Rd. (illustrated on the right)

20 Second-widest diameter tulip tree street tree in Seattle: 2016 NE Ravenna Blvd., at the entrance of "Candy Cane Lane"

Also see:

- **Fourth-widest diameter tulip tree street tree in Seattle:** Leschi (922 Davis Pl. S.)
- **Fifth-widest diameter tulip tree street tree in Seattle:** Capitol Hill (747 16th Ave. E.)
- **Seventh-widest diameter tulip tree street tree in Seattle:** Madison Park (3815 E. Garfield St.)
- **Eighth-widest diameter tulip tree street tree in Seattle:** Bryant (3311 NE 60th St.)
- **Mount Baker's widest diameter tulip tree street tree:** 2851 Mt. Rainier Dr. S.

A Deeper Dig

"A tulip tree which was a 'great disappointment' to Mrs. Axel Granstrom because it didn't bloom for 24 years, finally covered itself with tulip-like flowers the other day," reported the _Seattle Daily Times_ in 1950. The cul-de-sac known as Candy Cane Lane is home to two of the city's widest tulip street trees.

Douglas fir (*Pseudotsuga menziesii*)
4013 Bagley Ave. N.

WALLINGFORD *Firs*

Seattle's most famous fir is perhaps the Douglas fir, which is not a true fir at all (it is, rather, a false hemlock). For many, firs were the main reason to come to Seattle in the first place. They turned out to be the most economically and ecologically important tree species in history, and millions of seedlings have since been exported to every corner of the world, although the state of Washington remains home to some of the tallest specimens.

The state is also the record holder of the tallest *cut* Douglas fir: In 1950, when Northgate opened, one of the first covered malls in the United States, a 212-foot Douglas fir from Enumclaw—estimated to be 287 years old—was chosen to be the mall's official Christmas tree. It took almost an entire day to fell the tree, and the 70-mile journey back to Seattle was led by a police escort. The president of the Northgate Company, Jim Douglas, wrote that the Douglas fir Christmas tree "was the turning point for Northgate. Thereafter, no one questioned the future success of the project."

More than 70 years later, physical retail stores have given way to online shopping and Northgate Mall itself has been repurposed, but the 1950 Christmas tree is still recognized as the tallest in the world by Guinness World Records.

There are roughly 1,470 Douglas fir right-of-way trees in Seattle and 272 true fir; Wallingford is home to the most. Briefly known as Interlaken in the early 20th century, Wallingford was described by the mayor at the time as a "maize [sic] of undergrowth and stumps."

"the tree of resilience"
ABIES & PSEUDOTSUGA
EVERGREEN

Total True Firs: 272 (0.2% of all right-of-way trees in Seattle)

Total "False" Firs: 1,470 (0.9% of all right-of-way trees in Seattle)

Douglas Fir
(PSEUDOTSUGA MENZIESII)
Max Height: 415'

1" soft needles

- deeply furrowed, thick bark; "corky"

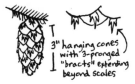

3" hanging cones with 3-pronged "bracts" extending beyond scales

NATIVE FROM BC TO MEXICO

1 Widest diameter Douglas fir in Wallingford: 4718 Burke Ave. N. on N. 48th St.

2 Second- and third-widest diameter Douglas fir street trees in Wallingford: 4013 Bagley Ave. N., a pair originally listed as "grand firs"

White Fir
(ABIES CONCOLOR)
Max Height: 250'

- rough bark, gray, ridged

2" flat needle, rounded tip

- drooping branches, flat top

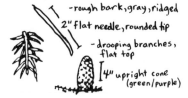

4" upright cone (green/purple)

FROM WESTERN N. AMERICA

3 Third-widest diameter true fir street tree in Seattle: 4520 Sunnyside Ave. N., a sad (but true) fir

Grand Fir
(ABIES GRANDIS)
Max Height: 206'

- flat ridged bark

1 3/4" needle, notched tip (2-ranked) (white line beneath)

- round-topped tree

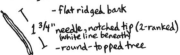

2 1/2" upright cones near tips of branches

Also see:

- **First-recorded Douglas fir street trees in Seattle:** N. Wedgwood (2502 NE 92nd St.)
- **Widest diameter Douglas fir street tree in Seattle:** Magnolia (3939 W. Barrett St.)
- **Second-widest diameter Douglas fir street tree in Seattle:** *Not illustrated:* Olympic Hills (13046 25th Ave. NE)
- **Third-widest diameter Douglas fir street tree in Seattle:** Ravenna (6818 19th Ave. NE)
- **Fourth-widest diameter Douglas fir street tree in Seattle:** Madrona/ Central District (528 30th Ave.)
- **Tied as fifth-widest diameter Douglas fir street tree in Seattle:** Phinney Ridge (6505 Woodland Pl. N. and 503 N. 64th St.)
- **Widest true fir street tree in Seattle:** *Not illustrated:* West Seattle, grand fir (3402 49th Ave. SW)
- **Second-widest grand fir street tree in Seattle:** Ravenna/South Wedgwood (6237 32nd Ave. NE)

Wallingford

other notable street trees :

American Persimmon
(DIOSPYROS VIRGINIANA)

-checkered bark; contorted

4½" oval leaf with pointed tip and wavy edges

1½" orange fruit (October)

④ **Widest diameter and second-widest diameter persimmon street trees in Seattle:** Wallingford, 1408 N. 47th St., two males incorrectly listed as "date-plum persimmon" in the city's data

Black Walnut
(JUGLANS NIGRA)

13–27 pointed leaflets (toothed)

-dark, furrowed bark

T 2" nut I

⑤ **Tied for 13th-widest diameter walnut street trees in Seattle:** 1818 N. 43rd St., next to a smaller gnarled English walnut

Cider Gum Eucalyptus
(EUCALYPTUS GUNNI)

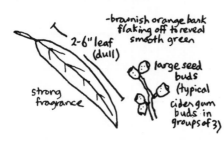

-brownish orange bark flaking off to reveal smooth green

2-6" leaf (dull)

strong fragrance

large seed buds (typical cider gum buds in groups of 3)

⑥ **Widest diameter eucalyptus street tree in Seattle:** 4228 Eastern Ave. N., shockingly planted only in 1991; listed only as "*Eucalyptus sp.*" in the city's data

Eastern Redbud
(CERCIS CANADENSIS)
Max Height: 66'

— multi-trunk tree

3½" heart-shaped leaf

—small pink flowers grow straight off trunk and branches (April to early June)

2½" brown seed pods

(7) Widest diameter redbud street tree in Seattle: 2305 N. 41st St., a pair on Corliss Ave. N.

European Chestnut
(CASTANEA SATIVA)

— short stalk

7" leaf with sharp teeth

white flower spikes (June to July)

spiky nut (late-September to early-October)

(8) First-recorded chestnut street tree in Seattle: 1609 N. 49th St.; listed on July 5, 1951, one month after the Washington State Ferries first began operation on Puget Sound; today, the agency has the largest fleet of passenger and auto ferries in the United States

Fig
(FICUS CARICA)
Max Height: 30'

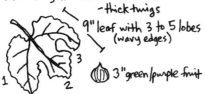

—thick twigs

9" leaf with 3 to 5 lobes (wavy edges)

3" green/purple fruit

(9) Second-widest diameter fig street tree in Seattle: 4515 Meridian Ave. N.

London Plane
(PLATANUS x ACERIFOLIA)

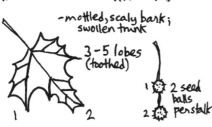

—mottled, scaly bark; swollen trunk

3-5 lobes (toothed)

1 2 seed balls
2 penstalk

(10) 11th-widest diameter plane street tree in Seattle: 2219 N. 46th St.

Loquat
(ERIOBOTRYA JAPONICA)
Max Height: 40'

7" to 16" glossy, leathery, wrinkled leaf with brown fuzz underneath

2" orange fruit (edible late spring to early-summer)

6" cluster of white, fragrant flowers (August-January)

11 Widest diameter loquat street tree in Seattle: 4207 Woodlawn Ave. N.; there are only 13 loquat right-of-way trees in the city and none come close to even half the size of the widest

Paper Birch
(BETULA PAPYRIFERA)

-white bark peeling at edge

3½" oval leaf (double-toothed) 5-10 pairs of veins

pendent catkins

12 Fourth-widest diameter paper birch street tree in Seattle: 2202 N. 41st St., on Bagley Ave. N.

Southern Catalpa
(CATALPA BIGNONIOIDES)

long stak

-scaly bark

7" heart-shaped leaf

2" bell-shaped flower (July to August)

10" seed pod

13 Second-widest diameter catalpa street tree in Seattle: 3614 Bagley Ave. N.

Western Red Cedar
(THUJA PLICATA)

-reddish, fibrous bark; often fluted and buttressed

- lacy scale-like foliage

⅓" upright cone

14 Tied as third-widest diameter Western red cedar street tree in Seattle: 4515 Woodlawn Ave. N.

Silk Tree
(ALBIZIA JULIBRISSIN)
Max Height: 60'

—umbrella-shaped tree

—lacy leaf with many sub-leaflets (folds up at night!)

5" fruit pod

pink puffs of flowers (late-July to late-September)

(15) Widest diameter silk tree street tree in Seattle (also a Heritage Tree): 3827 Bagley Ave. N.

Also see:
- **Second-widest diameter silk tree street tree in Seattle:** Greenwood (332 NW 79th St.)
- **Third-widest diameter silk tree street tree in Seattle:** Phinney Ridge (4903 2nd Ave. NW)
- **Only silk street tree in Eastlake:** 2225 Minor Ave. E.

Norway spruce (*Picea abies*)
9201 35th Ave. NE

North
WEDGWOOD
SPRUCE

In 1928, Mrs. George Adrian Smith, a prolific tree-planter associated with several local clubs including the Seattle Federation of Women's Clubs, advocated for planting a Norway Spruce at the club's home on Capitol Hill at Harvard Avenue East and East Thomas Street. At the dedication, she was quoted as saying, "In planting this hardy, dust-and-smoke-proof spruce we are giving growing space to a tree that one day will be tall and beautiful." (Today in 2023, the tree is neither tall, beautiful, or there at all). Future spruce street trees were not so lauded. In 1960, a Seattleite tried to plant one in his parking strip but was, according to the *Seattle Daily Times*, "denied by the Board of Public Works because evergreens are not approved for street plantings." The *Seattle Daily Times* reported that one citizen commented, aghast, "And this is the Evergreen State!"

Dating from the Cretaceous period, spruce can endure extreme heat and cold, and atmospheres with little oxygen or too much carbon dioxide. The boreal spruce forests of Alaska and Canada produce vast amounts of oxygen and absorb significant carbon, while they are also thought to have a direct relationship with the rainfall in the Great Plains of the US Midwest. (Sadly, one-seventh of Canada's boreal spruce forest has been clear-cut since 1990, mostly used as pulp for toilet paper.)

District 5, where north Wedgwood is located, has the most spruce right-of-way trees in the city. Unlike south Wedgwood, the area to the north wasn't absorbed into Seattle until 1953.

Spruce "the tree of farewell"
PICEA
EVERGREEN
Total: 576 (0.3% of all right-of-way trees in Seattle)

needles encircle twigs

gray, "scaly" bark →

Colorado Spruce
(PICEA PUNGENS)
Max Height: 159'

- twigs relatively thick
1" prickly blue-ish needle (with angles when rolled)

- conical, broad tree (branches sometimes drooping)

2-5" cone with wavy-tipped scales

FROM COLORADO'S ROCKY MOUNTAINS

(1) 9720 44th Ave. NE

(2) 3045 NE 86th St., flanking front steps; listed as only "spruce"

Norway Spruce
(PICEA ABIES)
Max Height: 226'

3/4" rigid needle; not prickly

- drooping twigs

4-9" cone with jagged-tipped scales

FROM EUROPE, RUSSIA

(3) **Widest diameter spruce street tree in Seattle:** 9201 35th Ave. NE, next to fence on NE 92nd St., listed only as "spruce"

Sitka Spruce
(PICEA SITCHENSIS)
Max Height: 317'
- broad crown

7/8" prickly, 4-angled needles (flattened) with white bands underneath

2-4" cone with pointed, toothed scales

NATIVE FROM S. ALASKA TO N. CALIFORNIA

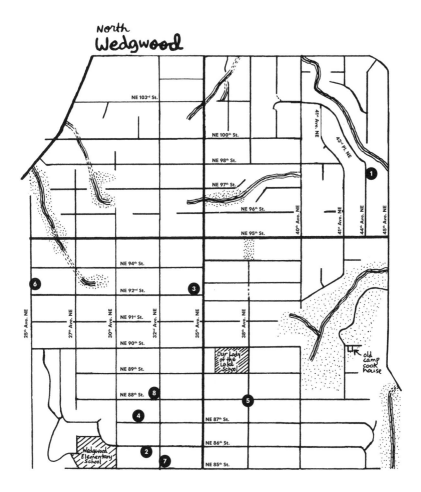

Also see:

- **Second-widest diameter spruce street tree in Seattle:** Queen Anne, Norway spruce (1007 W. Fulton St.)
- **Third-widest diameter spruce street tree in Seattle:** Ravenna, Norway spruce (1253 NE 69th St.)
- **Widest diameter Sitka spruce street tree in Seattle:** Green Lake (321 NE 57th St.)
- **First-recorded spruce street tree in Seattle:** Maple Leaf, Norway spruce (8535 4th Ave. NE)

other notable street trees:

Black Locust
(ROBINIA PSEUDOACACIA)

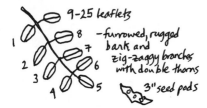

9-25 leaflets
-furrowed, rugged bark and zig-zaggy branches with double thorns
3" seed pods

❹ **Tied for second-widest diameter black locust street tree in Seattle:** 3022 NE 87th St., next to driveway

Camperdown Elm
(ULMUS 'CAMPERDOWNII')

-weeping branches
-"mop-headed" tree
-rough, toothed leaf; very lopsided

❺ **City's youngest and only Camperdown elm street tree in a traffic circle:** NE 88th St. & 38th Ave. NE

Douglas Fir
(PSEUDOTSUGA MENZIESII)

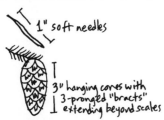

1" soft needles

3" hanging cones with 3-pronged "bracts" extending beyond scales

❻ **First-recorded Douglas fir street trees in Seattle:** 2502 NE 92nd St., unusual multi-trunked specimens on 25th Ave. NE, listed on July 29, 1958—the same day President Dwight D. Eisenhower signed the National Aeronautics and Space Act, creating NASA

Western Red Cedar
(THUJA PLICATA)

⅓" cone
-reddish, fibrous bark, often fluted and buttressed
-lacy scale-like foliage

❼ 3202 NE 85th St., multi-trunked specimens in right-of-way on 32nd Ave. NE; listed on July 7, 1979, the same day "coinless pay phones" made their debut in Seattle allowing callers to use a credit card

Eastern White Pine
(PINUS STROBUS)

3-5" needles
(bundles of 5)

4-8" narrow cone with long stalk (hangs in clusters)

- furrowed gray bark

8 **Widest-diameter pine "street tree" in Seattle:** 3054 NE 88th St., on corner obstructing front steps; the owner reported the previous neighbors who grew up at the house in the 1970s remembered that they used a branch of the pine to swing from their lawn down to the sidewalk

south
WEDGWOOD
oak

Civilization has prospered where oaks grew, with the wood providing the means to make everything from ships to barrels. The Oregon white oak, a.k.a. the Garry oak, is the Pacific Northwest's only native oak species, yet without periodic fires, Garry oaks decline in numbers. Evidence shows that indigenous people near present-day Seward Park knew this and would set deliberate wildfires to perpetuate the natural cycle, encouraging the growth of food sources. After settlers arrived in Seattle, much of the Garry oak habitat was turned into pasture, while fire suppression made it untenable for existing Garry oaks to survive.

In 1957, in early preparation for the Seattle World's Fair, the Seattle City Council approved plantings of nonnative northern red oak street trees downtown on Fourth Avenue from Virginia Street to Denny Way. A landscape architect "urged speed to ensure proper growth by fair time in 1961." By 1977, the gardening editor of the *Seattle Daily Times* was able to boast, "Oak trees are relatively easy to cultivate in this region."

But, while nonnative oaks have thrived, by the 1990s, more than half of our native oak's habitat in the Puget Sound region was gone.

There are roughly 7,000 oak street trees in Seattle, overall responsible for removing two million pounds of carbon dioxide from our atmosphere each year. District 4, where south Wedgwood is located, has the most.

Scarlet oak (*Quercus coccinea*)
7702 38th Ave. NE

oak // "the tree of bravery"
QUERCUS
DECIDUOUS (SOME EVERGREEN)
Total: 7,061 (4% of all right-of-way trees in Seattle)

California Valley Oak
(QUERCUS LOBATA)
Max Height: 178'
- spreading tree
- 4" leathery leaf, shiny on top
- gray, scaly or checkered bark
- 2" large acorn

FROM CALIFORNIA

1 Widest diameter valley oak street tree in Seattle (out of only six total in the city): 6058 36th Ave. NE, on NE 62nd St.

English Oak
(QUERCUS ROBUR)
Max Height: 150'
- ears on very short stalks
- 4½" round-lobed leaf with "eared" base
- thin stalk, 2" long
- 7/8" acorns (mid-August to September)

FROM EUROPE, N. AFRICA, CAUCUSES

2 27th Ave. NE & NE 60th St., traffic circle

Holm Oak
(QUERCUS ILEX)
Max Height: 131'
- smooth gray bark
- 2½" variably-shaped, leathery "holly-like" leaves
- underleaf fuzzy
- 1" acorn with deep cap and nipple-shaped tip

EVERGREEN • FROM MEDITERRANEAN TO W. HIMILAYAS

3 Widest diameter holm oak street trees in Seattle: 5727 28th Ave. NE, a pair

Pin Oak
(QUERCUS PALUSTRIS)
Max Height: 135'
- relatively smooth bark; fissures
- 5½" deeply-lobed leaf
- upright, narrow form with drooping lower branches
- 5/8" tiny acorns

FROM CENTRAL AND EASTERN N. AMERICA

4 12th-widest diameter oak street tree in Seattle: 6819 24th Ave. NE

Wedgwood

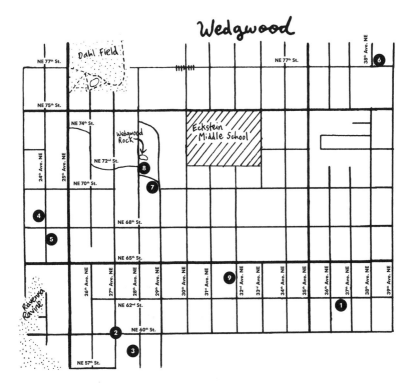

Red Oak
(QUERCUS RUBRA)
Max Height: 165'

- deep, broad, smooth ridged bark

7" shallow-lobed leaf, often with red stem

1" shallow-capped acorns

Scarlet Oak
(QUERCUS COCCINEA)
Max Height: 181'

- rougher bark than Pin Oak

6" deeply-lobed leaf

¾" deeply-capped acorns

FROM CENTRAL AND EASTERN N. AMERICA

5 **Second-widest diameter oak street tree in Seattle:** 6558 24th Ave. NE

FROM EASTERN UNITED STATES

6 **Widest diameter oak street tree in Seattle:** 7702 38th Ave. NE, at corner

7 **Ninth-widest diameter oak street tree in Seattle:** 7007 29th Ave. NE, several

Scarlet oak (Quercus coccinea)
7702 38th Ave. NE

Also see:

- **Third- and fifth-widest diameter oak street tree in Seattle:** NW Queen Anne, pin oaks (2667 10th Ave. W.)
- **Fourth-widest diameter oak street tree in Seattle:** Cherry Hill, red oak (921 18th Ave.)
- **Tied as fifth-widest diameter oak street tree in Seattle:** Greenwood, red oak (150 NW 80th St.)
- **Tied as sixth-widest diameter oak street tree in Seattle:** West Seattle, English oak (5954 49th Ave. SW)
- **Tied as seventh-widest diameter oak street tree in Seattle:** University District, pin oak (5806 16th Ave. NE)
- **Tied as eighth-widest diameter oak street tree in Seattle:** West Seattle, pin oak (2123 47th Ave. SW)
- **Widest diameter Garry oak in right-of-way in Seattle:** *Not illustrated:* East Capitol Hill, Garry oak (730 Belmont Ave. E.)
- **First-recorded oak street trees in Seattle:** Phinney Ridge, pin oak (5613 Greenwood Ave. N.)
- **First-recorded street trees in downtown:** red oaks (2001 4th Ave.)
- **Widest diameter Garry oak street tree in a planting strip in Seattle:** *Not illustrated:* Madison Valley (1432 29th Ave.)

WEDGWOOD (South)
other notable street trees:

Atlas Cedar
(CEDRUS ATLANTICA)

8 7200 28th Ave. NE, squished up
next to a massive glacial boulder

- horizontal branching

3/4" silvery-blue needles
in bunches along
branches

round, squat
cones

A Deeper Dig

In the late 1880s, the glacial erratic, known today as the
"Wedgwood Rock," became part of a 160-acre land claim "in a
dense forest." Edmond S. Meany, one of the first graduates of
the University of Washington, brought students to learn about
geology at the rock in the 20th century, and Lloyd Anderson,
the founder of REI, regularly brought members of Seattle's
Mountaineers Club to practice climbing it.

The neighborhood around the rock was developed in the
1940s, with the developer promising "not to touch the rock" as
part of the agreement. In the 1970s, hippies described as "dirty,
long-haired, bearded individuals" reportedly loitered around it,
causing the Seattle City Council to pass an ordinance making it
a crime to climb the rock, punishable by a fine of $100.

Grand Fir
(ABIES GRANDIS)
Max Height: 300'

-round topped tree; flat ridged bark

1 ³/₄" needle, notched tip with white bands underneath (2-ranked on branch)

2 ¹/₂" upright cone

9 **Second-widest diameter grand fir street tree in Seattle:** 6237 32nd Ave. NE, planted by owner in the late 1970s as a "living Christmas tree" for her children

Power Struggles

The concept of utility poles was first introduced by Samuel Morse (of Morse Code fame) who used them to erect telegraph wires in 1844, with the first message transmitted reading: "What hath God wrought?" There are approximately 91,000 utility poles maintained by Seattle City Light and many street trees were first planted in Seattle when there were few, if any, utility poles at all.

Over the course of the 20th century, new amenities like telephones, air conditioners, refrigerators, TVs, and wireless internet required an increasing amount of electricity and connections while, in parallel, our street trees matured. Many grew as high as the power lines or even higher, sometimes interfering with high-voltage transmissions. The resulting conflict is part of the reason why trees cause half of all power outages in Seattle.

A dedicated Power Line Clearance team attempts to keep hazards clear by employing methods such as "directional" and "side" pruning, leaving street trees mohawked, Pac-Man-ed, and guillotined. To see the casualties, you need not walk far. Mutilated shade and evergreen trees appear on nearly every block. "The truth of the matter is there are no nice solutions to the problem of trees growing into power lines," admitted Cass Turnbull, founder of the nonprofit PlantAmnesty. "Power line clearance workers are caught between a rock and a hard place, and the situation mirrors many of our current political and social problems."

"V" pruning   "Directional" Pruning   Side Pruning   Crown Reduction

WEST SEATTLE
yew

Yews made such important sacred sites in pagan religions that when Christianity spread in the Middle Ages, in an effort to build on familiar traditions, churches in Europe chose to strategically construct near the local yew tree rather than other locations, which is why graveyards are peppered with legendary English yews that are thousands of years old and often predate the churches themselves. Due to the yew's unique regenerative qualities, the true age of these trees is impossible to know because traditional methods of estimation such as ring counting cannot be used.

There are only 71 yew right-of-way trees in the city, most mere bushes with only 14 of those locations in planting strips. West Seattle is home to only one, but it happens to be the widest and only proper tree-sized yew street tree in the entire city. White settlers, led by Arthur Denny, first landed in present-day West Seattle at Alki Point in November 1851. Aghast at what Denny described later to be "as wild a spot as any on earth," the women in Denny's party reportedly wept and begged to move to another location—which Denny acquiesced to after a few miserable winter months, moving most of the group to the more sheltered area of present-day Pioneer Square. (Those who remained at Alki eventually also gave up by 1868, joining the others in present-day Downtown.)

English yew (*Taxus baccata*)
2616 50th Ave. SW

yew
"the tree of immortality"
TAXUS
EVERGREEN
Total: 71 (0.5% of all right-of-way trees in Seattle)

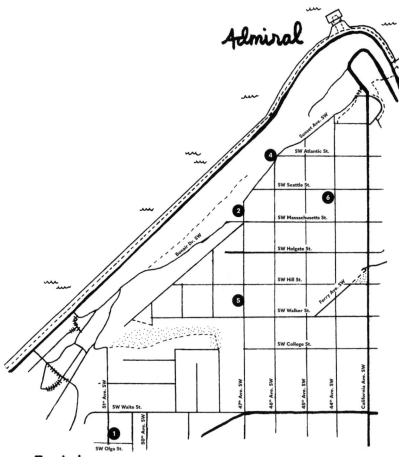

Admiral

English
Yew
(TAXUS BACCATA)

- reddish brown bark, peeling
  scales; fluted trunk
1" shiny needles
  (Pacific Yew is abruptly
    pointed while
    English Yew is
    gradually tapered)
  red berries ♀

1 Widest diameter yew street tree in Seattle (out of only 71 total): 2616 50th Ave. SW

WEST SEATTLE
other notable street trees:

Coast Redwood
(SEQUOIA SEMPERVIRENS)

1" needles, feathery

yellowish pollen cones

1" cone

2 Widest diameter coast redwood street tree in a planting strip in Seattle: 1627 Sunset Ave. SW

3 Third-widest diameter coast redwood street tree in a planting strip in Seattle: 5956 37th Ave. SW, on SW Raymond St.

English Elm
(ULMUS PROCERA)

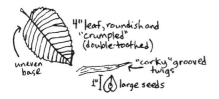

4" leaf, roundish and "crumpled" (double-toothed)

uneven base

"corky" grooved twigs

1" large seeds

4 Second- and sixth-widest diameter elm street trees in Seattle: 1439 Sunset Ave. SW; listed incorrectly as "American elm"

WEST SEATTLE
Morgan Junction

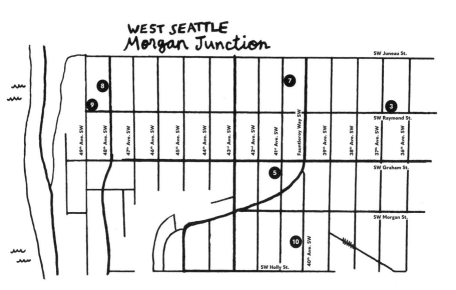

Pin Oak
(QUERCUS PALUSTRIS)

-upright, narrow tree with drooping lower branches and relatively smooth bark

5 ½" deeply-lobed leaf

⬤ ⏋ ⁵⁄₈" tiny acorns

5 Tied as eighth-widest diameter oak street tree in Seattle: 2123 47th Ave. SW

Western Red Cedar
(THUJA PLICATA)

-red, fibrous bark
- fluted and buttressed trunk

- lacy scale-like foliage

⏉ ⅓" upright cone with toothed scales

6 Tied as third-widest diameter western red cedar street tree in Seattle: 4403 SW Seattle St., on 44th Ave. SW

European Chestnut
(CASTANEA SATIVA)

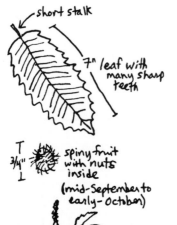

← short stalk

7" leaf with many sharp teeth

⏉ ¾" spiny fruit with nuts inside
(mid-September to early-October)

♂ male flowers in white spikes (June to July)

7 Seventh-widest diameter European chestnut street tree in Seattle: 5922 41st Ave. SW, pair listed incorrectly in the city's data as American chestnut

Black Locust
(ROBINIA PSEUDOACACIA)

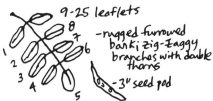

9-25 leaflets

-rugged furrowed bark; zig-zaggy branches with double thorns

-3" seed pod

8 Tied for third-widest diameter black locust street tree in Seattle: 5945 48th Ave. SW

English Oak
(QUERCUS ROBUR)

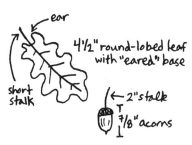

ear

4½" round-lobed leaf with "eared" base

short stalk

← 2" stalk

⊥ ⅞" acorns

9 Tied as sixth-widest diameter oak street tree in Seattle: 5954 49th Ave. SW, on SW Raymond St.

Giant Sequoia
(SEQUOIADENDRON GIGANTEUM)

- cord-like twigs
- reddish, fibrous bark

2½" cone

10 Widest diameter giant sequoia tree in the public right-of-way in Seattle (also a Heritage Tree): 6531 40th Ave. SW, in yard next to sidewalk

City's first-recorded street trees in a planting strip: 3531 SW Monroe St.; four listed on July 2, 1950, the same year Northgate Mall opened, the nation's first postwar shopping center referred to as a "shopping mall"; it has since been redeveloped as a mixed-use complex.

WEST SEATTLE
(Part of)
Fauntleroy

SW Holden St.

| 36ᵗʰ Ave. SW | 35ᵗʰ Ave. SW | 34ᵗʰ Ave. SW | Roxhill Elementary |

SW Kenyon St.

SW Monroe St.

SW Elmgrove St.

English Midland Hawthorn
(CRATAEGUS LAEVIGATA)

2" leaf

- reddish-pink, fragrant flowers (10+ petals); blooms earlier than other Hawthorns, May to June
- scaly, fluted trunk

½ red fruit (2-3 seeds)

241

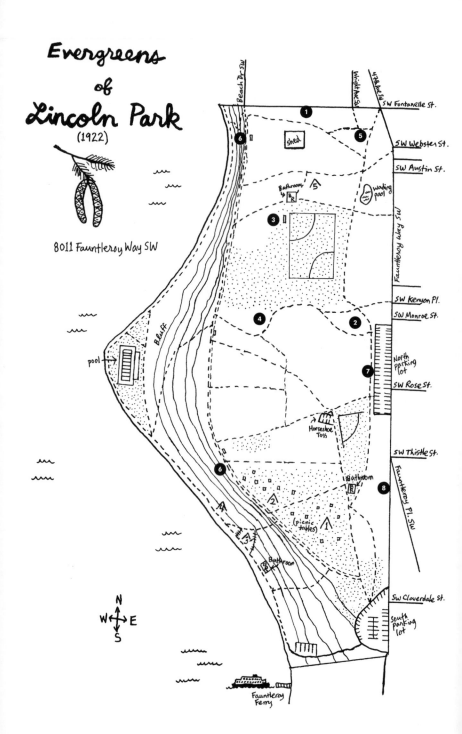

Evergreens
of
Lincoln Park
(1922)

8011 Fauntleroy Way SW

shed

Beach Dr SW

Wright Ave S.

47th Ave SW

SW Fontanelle St.

SW Webster St.

SW Austin St.

Bathroom

wading pool

Fauntleroy Way SW

SW Kenyon Pl.

SW Monroe St.

North parking lot

SW Rose St.

pool

Bluff

Horseshoe Toss

SW Thistle St.

Fauntleroy Pl. SW

Bathroom

(picnic tables)

Bathroom

SW Cloverdale St.

South parking lot

N
W   E
S

Fauntleroy Ferry

242

① Bay laurel (*Laurus nobilis*)
North of northern path, bay laurel leaves are fragrant
when crushed and used in cooking (yellow flowers late
March to early May)

② Coast redwood (*Sequoia sempervirens*)
A grove of around 30 northwest of northern parking lot

③ Douglas fir (*Pseudotsuga menziesii*)
Two at the northwest corner of the baseball field
behind the bleachers

④ Incense cedar (*Calocedrus decurrens*)
A grove southwest of baseball field

⑤ Japanese cedar (*Cryptomeria japonica*)
A multi-trunked tree in the northeast corner of the
park, west of the path (with reddish bark, short and
prickly needle-like foliage, and spiky, round 1" cones)

⑥ Pacific madrona (*Arbutus menziesii*)
Many of this red-barked tree along the cliffs near
benches in northwest corner of park and also along
southern bluff path

⑦ Ponderosa pine (*Pinus ponderosa*)
Several on west side of northern parking lot

⑧ Western red cedar (*Thuja plicata*)
A grove east of the south restrooms on the east
park border

Deciduous Trees

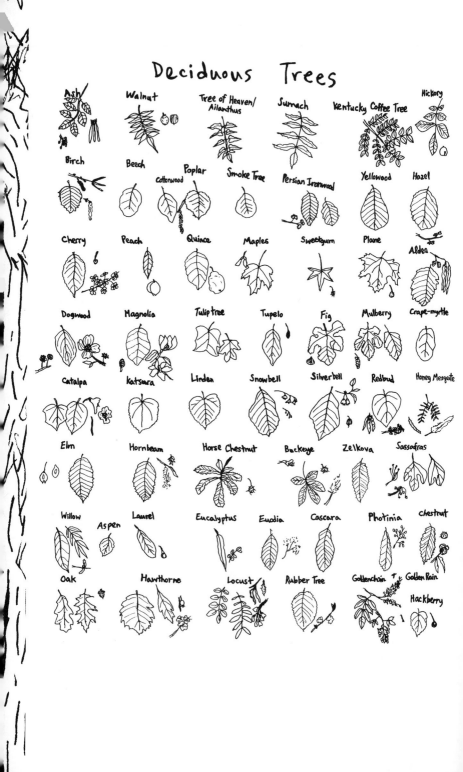

Afterword

Street trees are particularly challenged—often planted far from their native homes, constricted in how far they can spread, lacking legacy information from older trees present in natural forests, and weakened by pollution. They are paragons of resilience and endurance, and take years to grow canopies, develop relationships, host other life, and establish roots. When an older tree is cut down, there is no such thing as immediate replacement. Even replacing one mature tree with multiple young trees cannot make up for the loss of the specific diversity of life that one tree may have built over decades. In fact, researchers have discovered that larger street trees provide *10 times* the human well-being benefits.

Recent extreme heat waves in the Pacific Northwest have made the importance of our urban forest even more immediately tangible, with treeless paved landscapes up to 20 degrees Fahrenheit hotter in a city where air-conditioning is still scarce. Nationwide, low-income neighborhoods and communities of color have significantly less tree canopy, with the wealthiest neighborhoods home to 65 percent more street trees than the lowest-income areas. American horticulturist Furman Lloyd Mulford observed in 1920, "If it is impossible to grow trees on a street, as a health measure that street should be closed for human use until conditions are so improved that it will support trees." A century later, the absence of street trees is still a symbol of poverty, powerlessness, and neglect.

Following the 2008 recession in the United States, funds for urban tree maintenance were severely limited, and many cities shifted maintenance and liability for street trees to private property owners. We have since discovered that a tree can provide benefits to anyone within a third of a mile radius (roughly three blocks), impacting a community beyond a single private property owner. In 2023, approximately 70 percent of Seattle's street trees were privately maintained, under municipal regulation.

Street trees are an evolving experiment, a bellwether for what is to come. Lacking the adequate funds to maintain all its street trees and the policies to protect those trees still standing, the City of Seattle encourages residents to plant trees along public streets on their own. Each household is eligible for four free trees with a lifetime maximum of six trees. The city provides training on tree selection, proper planting, and care, but private owners assume all further responsibility.

The amorphous space a street tree occupies is where people experience the same events and passing seasons. This hidden forest is where our shared stories develop: As our trees disappear, so does our understanding of the past, our connection to each other.

To date, protection for trees is fraught and altogether incommensurate with their long-term value as part of a city's climate resilience infrastructure. Clearing every inconvenient street tree on the block is often the first step of any new development or renovation. As urban density neccessarily increases, it is now more important than ever to remember that all housing can and should be physically and psychologically healthy also.

Acknowledgments

This book is a physical manifestation of how I spent the pandemic years, an artifact of the strange times we lived through. As borders closed and flights ceased, many of us survived thanks to our newly hyper-local communities. I have these people to thank: Lele Barnett, Tom Butcher, Ryan Anthony Donaldson, Katie Davies and Marissa Hiller accompanied me on far too many epic walks. Arthur Lee Jacobson helped me validate trees and gamely answered my endless questions, inviting me into his world. Numerous people (some of whom I never met in person) generously helped confirm trees I could not visit in person, including Barbara Bernard, Weston Brinkley, Josh Morris, Kersti Muul, Stuart Niven and Sandy Shettler. Others read drafts and shared books, research and encouragement, including Kathy Ackerman, Knute Berger, Andy Cotgreave, Erie Edwin Jones, Jess and Sean Hennessy, Anne Knight, Jocelyn Malheiro, Alice Marwick, Sue Nicol, Lee O'Connor, Jennifer Ott, Dan Shepherd, Terry Surguine and David B. Williams. I am eternally grateful to the team at Sasquatch Books, including the inimitable Jen Worick, the ever-patient Isabella Hardie, and the very talented Tony Ong. And, of course, I'd be remiss not to thank my dear parents who have always believed anything is possible—my mom, Nahid Rouhfar, and my dad, Yaghoob Ebrahimi (for them, I dedicate this book "for Valiasr St. and its forlorn trees").

References

General

Lawrence, Henry W. *City Trees: A Historical Geography from the Renaissance through the Nineteenth Century*. Charlottesville: University of Virginia Press, 2006.

West, David and Hobbs, Kevin. *The Story of Trees: And How They Changed the Way We Live*. London: Laurence King, 2020.

Scott, Michael. *The Tree Book: The Stories, Science, and History of Trees*. London: Smithsonian, 2022.

"Allied Arts Acting as Esthetic Lobbyist." *Seattle Daily Times*, May 9, 1976.

Krenmayr, Janice. "Street Trees: For Beauty and Other Benefits." *Seattle Times Magazine*, March 31, 1974.

Mitchell, Alan. *Trees of Britain & Northern Europe*. London: HarperCollins, London, 1982.

Johnson, Owen. *British Tree Guide*. London: William Collins, 2004.

Jacobson, Arthur Lee. *Trees of Seattle*. Seattle: Sasquatch Books, 1989.

Wohlleben, Peter. *The Hidden Life of Trees*. Vancouver, BC: Greystone Books, 2015.

Simard, Suzanne. *Finding the Mother Tree*. New York: Alfred A. Knopf, 2021.

Dümpelmann, Sonja. *Seeing Trees: A History of Street Trees in New York City and Berlin*. New Haven: Yale University Press, 2019.

Dietz, Theresa S. *The Complete Language of Flowers*. New York: Wellfleet, 2020.

Sibley, David. *The Sibley Guide to Trees*. New York: Alfred A. Knopf, 2009.

Rawlence, Ben. *The Treeline: The Last Forest and the Future of Life on Earth*. New York: St. Martin's, 2022.

Jonnes, Jill. *Urban Forests: A Natural History of Trees and People in the American Cityscape*. New York: Penguin Books, 2017.

Willix, Douglas. "Council Committee Recommends Long Tree-Planting Plan." *Seattle Daily Times*, May 24, 1966.

O'Neil-Dunne, Jarlath. 2016 Seattle Tree Canopy Assessment. City of Seattle Trees for Seattle.

"Trees for Seattle." City of Seattle Official Website.

Morris, Joshua. "Exploring Seattle's Urban Forest." *Seattle Audubon*, May 2, 2019.

Webber, Simone. "Technical Note—How Do Trees Store Carbon?" *Creating Tomorrow's Forests*, May 23, 2022.

Tadewaldt, Lisa. "Beware of Sudden Branch Drop." *Urban Forest Pro*, October 4, 2022.

Serafin, Amelia, and Brooke Wynalda. "Trees Take the Streets: Urban Tree Growth and Hazard Potential." *SUURJ: Seattle University Undergraduate Journal 5*, article 12, 2021.

Schmidlin, Thomas W. "Human Fatalities from Wind-Related Tree Failures in the United States, 1995–2007." *Natural Hazards 50* (2009): 13–25.

Turnbull, Cass. "Power Lines." PlantAmnesty.

Beer, Amy-Jane. "A Tree a Day." San Francisco: Chronicle Books, 2022.

Baker, Ken. "Non-Virtual Reality: Do You Ever Notice the Forest of Utility Poles?" *Fremont News Messenger*, January 15, 2019.

Galle, Nadina. "Talking Trees—Part 1: Do City Trees Talk to Each Other?" *Internet of Nature* (blog), February 11, 2021.

Higgins, Adrian. "The Battle of Power Lines and the Urban Forest." *Washington Post*, August 15, 2012.

Beery, Sara. "Mapping Urban Trees Across North America with the Auto Arborist Dataset." Google Research, June 22, 2022.

"Trees Serve As Speed Bumps for Rain." Restore Our Waters, City of Seattle.

Mapes, Lynda V. and Mayor, Justin, "A Fight for Urban Trees: Seattle's Wealthier Neighborhoods Leafier." *Seattle Times*, August 13, 2014.

Dougherty, Phil. "Interstate 5 Is Completed in Washington on May 14, 1969." HistoryLink.org, April 10, 2010.

Williams, David B. *Too High and Too Steep: Reshaping Seattle's Topography*. Seattle: University of Washington Press, 2015.

Donovan, Geoffrey H. "The Relationship Between Trees and Human Health: Evidence from Spread of the Emerald Ash Borer." *American Journal of Preventive Medicine*, Vol 44, Issue 2, February 2013.

City of Seattle Official Website. "Trees for Seattle, Regulations, Do I Need a Permit? Planting Trees."

Dengkai, Chi, et al., "Residential Exposure to Urban Trees and Medication Sales for Mood Disorders and Cardiovascular Disease in Brussels, Belgium: An Ecological Study." *Environmental Health Perspectives*, Volume 130, No. 5. May 11, 2022.

Rojas-Rueda, David, et al., "Green Spaces and Mortality: A Systematic Review and Meta-analysis of Cohort Studies." *Lancet Planet Health*, November 3, 2019.

"What's a Street Tree?" Trees for Seattle, City of Seattle Official Website.

Galle, Nadina. Personal interview with Taha Ebrahimi, November 1, 2022.

Rundquist, Nolan. Email correspondence with Taha Ebrahimi, December 21, 2022.

Banel, Feliks. "Cherry trees in front of Pike Place Market are gone." MyNorthwest KIRO NewsRadio, March 14, 2023.

Brown, Alex. "A cool idea for low-income urban areas hit by warming climate: More trees." *The Washington Post*, July 12, 2021.

Mahoney, Sally Gene. "Tree experiment: before the fall." *Seattle Daily Times*, January 29, 1977.

Varney, Val. "Budget cuts may trim planting of trees in city." *Seattle Daily Times*, July 23, 1975.

2021 City of Seattle Tree Canopy Assessment. University of Vermont Spatial Analysis Lab, City of Seattle Office of Sustainability and Environment.

"Trees." Seattle Department of Transportation, Urban Forestry. City of Seattle GIS Program, Seattle GeoData (Open Data): Accessed 2020.

"ds002-trees (Data Stories: Seattle's Street Tree Inventory)." [Tableau Public data visualization] Seattle Department of Transportation, February 7, 2021.

Demay, Danial. "The Northwest's logging heritage." *The Seattle Post-Intelligencer*, January 21, 2016.

US Environmental Protection Agency. *Report to Congress on indoor air quality: Volume II: Assessment and Control on Indoor Air Pollution*. Washington, DC, August 1989.

Klepeis, Neil. "The National Human Activity Pattern Survey (NHAPS): a resource for assessing exposure to environmental pollutants" *Journal of Exposure Science and Epidemiology*, July 26, 2001.

US Census Bureau, "Urban Areas Facts," October 8, 2021.

Weinberger, Hannah. "You might be responsible for a Seattle street tree and not know it." *Crosscut*, April 12, 2003.

Seattle Department of Transportation. "Seattle's Street Tree Inventory." Accessed February 7, 2021.

In addition to what is noted in the general references, the following sources were consulted for neighborhood chapters:

Ballard | Cherry (*Prunus*)

Asaka, Megan. *Seattle from the Margins*. Seattle: University of Washington Press, 2022.

Consulate-General of Japan in Seattle. "The History of Trade between Washington State and Japan," last updated May 3, 2022.

Crowley, Walt. "Seattle Neighborhoods: Ballard—Thumbnail History." HistoryLink.org, March 31, 1999.

Daniels, Roger. *Asian America: Chinese and Japanese in the United States since 1850*. Seattle: University of Washington Press, 1988.

Grant, Nicole. "White Supremacy and the Alien Land Laws of Washington State." Seattle Civil Rights & Labor History Project, University of Washington.

Japan American Center Seattle: Seattle Cherry Blossom & Japanese Cultural Festival, "Celebrating Cherry Blossoms."

Kuitert, Wybe. *Japanese Flowering Cherries*. Portland, OR: Timber Press, 1999.

Liu, Marian. "Seattle Dojo Has Welcomed Generations of Families for More Than a Century." *Seattle Times*, June 15, 2008.

National Park Service, US Department of the Interior. "Cherry Blossom Festival: History of the Cherry Trees."

Nishinoiri, John. "Japanese Farms in Washington." Master's thesis, University of Washington, 1926.

Pacific Coast Architecture Database. "Seattle Cedar Lumber Manufacturing Company, Mill, Ballard, Seattle, WA."

Rademaker, John. "The Ecological Position of the Japanese Farmers in the State of Washington." PhD diss., University of Washington, 1939.

Seattle Municipal Archives. "Ballard."

Shiotani, Yuki. "History of the Cherry Trees in the Liberal Arts Quadrangle at the University of Washington." PhD diss., University of Washington, 2019.

Takaki, Ronald. *Strangers from a Different Shore: A History of Asian Americans*. New York: Little, Brown, 1989.

Takami, David A. *Divided Destiny: A History of Japanese Americans in Seattle*. Seattle: Wing Luke Asian Museum and University of Washington Press, 1998.

Takami, David. "Japanese Farming." HistoryLink.org, October 29, 1998.

Talbert, Paul. *Cherries, Lanterns, and Gates: Japanese and Japanese-American Cultural Gifts in Seattle Parks*. Seattle: Friends of Seward Park, 2011.

Yoon-Hendricks, Alexandra. "81 Years Ago, Japanese Americans Were Forced to Leave Bainbridge Island." *Seattle Times*, February 19, 2023.

Beacon Hill | Holly (*Ilex*)

Darrow, Katherine. "An Evergreen State of Mind: The Introduction of Holly to Washington's Forests; Nature Notes." *Leader*, January 31, 2023.

"The Story of English Holly: Not-So-Jolly Holly." *King County Noxious Weed News* (blog), December 23, 2021.

King County Noxious Weed Control Program. "English Holly Identification and Control." April 24, 2020.

Smith, Al. "How Washington Nearly Became the Holly State." *Douglasia*, Winter 2013.

Rurik, Kris. "Deck the Halls: When the KP Grew Holly." *Key Peninsula News*, December 2, 2021.

Watts, Andrea "English Holly: Garden and Wildlife Favorite or Invasive Foe?" *Pacific Horticulture*, October 2012.

Wilma, David. "Seattle Neighborhoods: Beacon Hill—Thumbnail History." HistoryLink.org, February 21, 2001.

Bryant | Monkey Puzzle Tree (*Araucaria*)

Paine, Edward. "The Monkey Puzzle—A Little History." *Last Frontiers* (blog), April 1, 2019.

"Seattle Public Schools, 1862–2000: William Cullen Bryant Elementary School." HistoryLink.org, August 28, 2013.

"Names in the Neighborhood: Bryant." *Wedgwood in Seattle History* (blog), November 1, 2021.

Wihman, Liisa. "The Pacific Connections of the Monkey Puzzle Tree." *Washington Park Arboretum Bulletin*, Winter 2012, 3–6.

Moody, Dick. "Monkey-Tree Seeds Are Hard to Find." *Seattle Daily Times*, February 10, 1975.

Moody, Dick. "Monkey-Tree Seeds." *Seattle Daily Times*, February 13, 1975.

Capitol Hill (Northeast) | Redwood (*Sequoia*)

Farrow, Roy. "December 2019 Plant Profile: Sequoia Sempervirens." University of Washington Botanical Gardens, December 5, 2019.

"Interlaken Park and Boulevard." Friends of Seattle's Olmsted Parks.

Szalay, Jessie. "Giant Sequoias and Redwoods: The Largest and Tallest Trees." *Live Science*, May 4, 2017.

Thorness, Bill. "125 Years Ago, Bicyclists Paved the Way for the Lake Washington. Path—Seattle's First Long, Paved Bike Path." *Seattle Times*, June 10, 2022.

Uitti, Jake. "Seattle's Giant Sequoia Tree." *Atlas Obscura*, May 2, 2018.

"City of Seattle, Parks and Recreation Department, Interlaken Park, Interlaken, Seattle, WA." Pacific Coast Architecture Database, 1905.

Matray, James I. "The Korean War 101: Causes, Course, and Conclusion of the Conflict." *Education About Asia*, Volume 17, Number 3, Winter 2012, 26.

Ferguson, Robert L. "Pioneers of Lake View: A Guide to Seattle's Early Settlers and Their Cemetery." *Thistle*, December 1, 1996.

Capitol Hill (Southeast) | Maple (*Acer*)

Sherrard, Jean. "The Finest Fruit." *Seattle Now & Then* (blog), July 18, 2014.

"State Officials Ask for Public's Help in Tracking the Invasive Tree-of-Heaven." Washington Recreation and Conservation Office, Washington Invasive Species Council, September 29, 2021.

"Statewide Call for Tree-of-Heaven Locations in Effort to Prevent Spotted Lanternfly Spread." *King County Noxious Weed News* (blog), October 12, 2021.

McNeur, Catherine. "The Tree That Still Grows in Brooklyn, and Almost Everywhere Else." Gotham Center for New York City History, January 4, 2018.

Stein, Alan J. "Lynch Mob Hangs Three Men in Seattle on January 18, 1882." HistoryLink.org, January 1, 2000.

Dorpat, Paul. "The Dark Day of Mob Rule and Lynching as Sport in Seattle" *Seattle Times*, July 18, 2014.

"Civil Defense for A-Bomb Readied." *Sweetwater Reporter* (Sweetwater, Tex.), Vol. 53, No. 221, Ed. 1 Monday, September 18, 1950, Page 1.

Malone, Patrick. "What Russia's Nuclear Escalation Means for Washington, with World's Third-Largest Atomic Arsenal" *Seattle Times*, March 12, 2022.

Ferguson, Robert L. "Pioneers of Lake View." *Thistle*, December 1, 1996.

Cherry Hill | Ash (*Fraxinus*)

Arden, Amanda. "Officials Prep for Invasive Emerald Ash Borer to Spread to Washington State." *KOIN 6 News*, July 26, 2022.

"Oregon Dad Spots the First Emerald Ash Borers on the West Coast during Summer Camp Pickup in Forest Grove." Oregon Department of Agriculture, July 11, 2022.

"Racial Restrictive Covenants: Neighborhood by Neighborhood Restrictions across King County." Seattle Civil Rights & Labor History Project, University of Washington.

Honig, Doug. "Redlining in Seattle." HistoryLink.org, October 29, 2021.

Henry, Mary T. "Seattle Neighborhoods: Central Area—Thumbnail History." HistoryLink.org, March 10, 2001.

Giles, Jeff. "'He Did All This Wild Playing': Behind the Scenes at Jimi Hendrix's First Ever Live Gig." *Classic Rock*, November 11, 2022.

"The Seattle Open Housing Campaign, 1959–1968." Seattle Municipal Archives.

"Tree-Cutting Mistake to Cost City $185." *Seattle Daily Times*, May 08, 1958.

Columbia City | Walnut (*Juglans*)

Tate, Cassandra. "Seattle Neighborhoods: Columbia City—Thumbnail History." HistoryLink.org, June 2, 2001.

"Growing Nut Trees." *Seattle Daily Times*, September 3, 1903.

List of old-growth forests, Wikipedia.

Tate, Cassandra. "Seward Park (Seattle)." HistoryLink.org, September 3, 2010.

Boak, Josh. "Climate Progress Remains Elusive for Biden on Earth Day." *Associated Press*, April 22, 2022.

Meier, Allison C. "The Ancient Forests That Have Defied Urbanization." *Bloomberg*, May 22, 2018.

Delridge | Madrone (*Arbutus*)

Elliott, Marianne. "Life and Death of Madrone in the PNW." Washington State University, 2020.

Salisbury, Nelson. "The State of Seattle's Madrone Forests." *Seattle Urban Nature*, 2008.

Dolan, Maria. "Madrona: Forgotten Native of the Northwest a Sight to Behold." *Seattle Times*, September 30, 2004.

Adams, A. D., ed. "The Decline of Pacific Madrone: (*Arbutus menziesii* Pursh): Current Theory and Research Directions." Center for Urban Horticulture, University of Washington, 1995.

Bentley, Judy. "Delridge History." Southwest Seattle Historical Society.

Young, Gerald. "The Pacific Madrone in the Salish Sea Ecosystem." *Salish Magazine*, Summer 2020.

Hamilton, Clement W. and West, Paul. "The Decline of Pacific Madrone: Current Theory and Research Directions." Proceedings of the April 28, 1995 Symposium Held at the Center for Urban Horticulture, University of Washington, xiii, xiv.

Dolan, Maria. "Madrona: Forgotten Native of the Northwest a Sight to Behold." *Seattle Times*, September 30, 2004.

Downtown | Plane (*Platanus*)

Editors. "City Affairs: Tree Protection." *Seattle Daily Times*, March 29, 1967.

Collins, Alf. "Trees Are Gone; Who's Stumped?" *Seattle Daily Times*, October 17, 1970.

Collins, Alf. "Activist and His Moveable Playground." *Seattle Daily Times*, November 7, 1976.

Mahoney, Sally Gene. "Street Trees Are Ripping and Tripping Things Up." *Seattle Daily Times*, December 24, 1978.

Gilmore, Susan. "Crowded Roots Put Downtown Sequoia in a Pinch." *Seattle Times*, June 18, 2010.

Lane, Polly. "Tree-Cutting Operation Branches into Ruckus." *Seattle Daily Times*, April 05, 1984.

Brown, Larry. "Uhlman Urges Triple Damages in Tree Cutting." *Seattle Daily Times*, November 19, 1970.

Hinterberger, John. "Students Replace Murdered Tree." *Seattle Daily Times*, October 20, 1970.

Crowley, Walt. "Seattle Neighborhoods: Downtown Seattle—Thumbnail History." HistoryLink.org, April 17, 1999.

Emery, Julie. "Mannhalt Convicted Again in Second Trial." *Seattle Times*, March 29, 1990.

Lane, Polly. "'Tree-Angle' for Downtown." *Seattle Daily Times*, April 02, 1972.

Steinbrueck, Victor. "Only the City Council Can Make a Tree." *Seattle Post-Intelligencer*, August 21, 1966.

"Hotel Elliot/Hahn Building." City of Seattle Landmarks Preservation Board, February 3, 2020.

Collins, Alf. "Trees Are Gone; Who's Stumped?" *Seattle Times*, October 17, 1970.

Wang, Yanan and Jenny Starrs. "'The Man in the Tree' Mesmerizes Seattle—from 80 Feet." *Washington Post*, March 23, 2016.

Steinbrueck, Victor. "Only the City Council Can Make a Tree." *Seattle Post-Intelligencer*, August 21, 1966: p. 80.

Eastlake | Willows (*Salix*)

Lacitis, Erik. "'It Has a Story to Tell': How a Descendant of Napoleon's Willow Tree Took Root on a Seattle Hillside." *Seattle Times*, October 29, 2018.

Sterling, E. M. "Spare Those Trees, the City Is Asked." *Seattle Daily Times*, February 20, 1966.

Fiset, Louis. "Seattle Neighborhoods: Eastlake—Thumbnail History." HistoryLink.org, May 5, 2001.

Fremont | Pines (*Pinus*)

Elman, Ella. "The State of Seattle's Conifers." Washington Department of Natural Resources: Seattle Urban Nature, 2009.

"The New Hampshire Pine Tree Riot of 1772." New England Historical Society.

Orlean, Susan. "The Tallest Known Tree in New York Falls in the Forest." *New Yorker*, January 18, 2022.

McRoberts, Patrick. "Seattle Neighborhoods: Fremont—Thumbnail History." HistoryLink.org, June 10, 1999.

"History of the Fremont Neighborhood in Seattle." *Wedgwood in Seattle History* (blog), May 1, 2015.

"Restoring Western White Pines in Idaho and Montana." USDA Forest Service Northern Region.

Georgetown | Locusts (*Robinia*)

Greene, Wesley. "Black Locust: The Tree on Which the US Was Built." *Live Science*, May 4, 2015.

Matarrese, Andy. "Sounding Alarm on Black Locust." *Columbian*, October 14, 2015.

Wilma, David. "Seattle Neighborhoods: Georgetown—Thumbnail History." HistoryLink.org, February 10, 2001.

Saltonstall, Dick. "Summer Is a Time of Poison Peril." *Seattle Daily Times*, June 26, 1964.

"Little Girl's Illness Prompts Warning on Poisonous Tree." *Seattle Daily Times*, May 18, 1960.

Saltonstall, Dick. "Danger to Children: Doctor Warns About Poison Plants." *Seattle Daily Times*, August 14, 1963.

Green Lake | Ginkgo (*Ginkgo*)

Cohn, Roger. "The Life Story of the Oldest Tree on Earth." *Yale Environment 360*, May 1, 2013.

Avis-Riordan, Katie. "Ginkgo Biloba: The Tree That Outlived the Dinosaurs." Royal Botanic Gardens, May 5, 2020.

Solly, Cecil. "Ginkgo Trees Grow Well Here." *Seattle Daily Times*, August 21, 1960.

Fiset, Louis. "Seattle Neighborhoods: Green Lake—Thumbnail History." HistoryLink.org, March 14, 2000.

Wingate, Marty. "NW Gardens: These Aren't Your Father's Street Trees" *Seattle Post-Intelligencer*, April 6, 2007.

Greenwood | Dogwood (*Cornus*)

"Would Plant Trees Along Seattle Streets." *Seattle Daily Times*, April 14, 1916.

"Sunset Club Hears Talk on Best Shrubs to Plant in the City." *Seattle Daily Times*, June 8, 1919.

Fiset, Louis. "Seattle Neighborhoods: Greenwood—Thumbnail History." HistoryLink.org, June 21, 2001.

Kroll's Atlas of Seattle, Washington. Seattle: Kroll Map Company, Inc., 1912, 1920.

Leschi | Apples & Crabapples (*Malus*)

Henry, David Thoreau. "Wild Apples: The History of the Apple-Tree." *Atlantic*, November 1862.

"Seattle Public Schools, 1862–2000: Martha Washington School for Girls." HistoryLink.org, September 9, 2013.

Wilma, David. "Martha Washington School." HistoryLink.org, March 21, 2001.

Lieberworth, Audrey L. "Seattle's Orchards: A Historic Legacy Meets Modern." Senior thesis, Claremont Colleges: Scripps College Senior Thesis, Sustainability. 2012.

Talbert, Paul. "History: SkEba'kst: The Lake People and Seward Park." Friends of Seward Park.

Sillman, Marcie. "Sweet Little Mysteries: Discovering Seattle's Hidden Orchards." KUOW, September 29, 2015.

Rochester, Junius. "Seattle Neighborhoods: Leschi—Thumbnail History." HistoryLink.org, July 11, 2001.

"Pacific Northwest Apples." Northwest Horticultural Council.

Culley, Theresa. "The Rise and Fall of the Ornamental Callery Pear Tree." Harvard Arboretum, *Arnolida*, Volume 74, Issue 3.

The Northwest Times, Volume 4, Number 7. January 21, 1950.

Nick McGurk. "Fans remember first Seahawks game, 40 years ago today." *KIRO 7*, August 1, 2016.

Higgins, Adrian. "Scientists Thought They Had Created the Perfect Tree. But it Became a Nightmare." *Washington Post*, October 26, 2018.

Sherrard, Jean. "He Opened Seattle's 1st Candy Shop—and Maybe Coined a Famous Ditty." *Seattle Times*, Oct. 13, 2022.

Loyal Heights | Eucalyptus (*Eucalyptus*)

Fiset, Louis. "Seattle Neighborhoods: Loyal Heights, Sunset Hill, and Shilshole—Thumbnail History." HistoryLink.org, July 8, 2001.

Irving, Ted. "On Growing Eucalypts in the Pacific Northwest." Pacific Horticulture.

Wrench, Robert. "Cultivated Eucalypts of Seattle and the Greater Pacific Northwest: A Field Guide." University of Washington, 2020.

Wingate, Marty. "Shaggy Eucalyptus: It's Not Just for Californians." *Seattle Post-Intelligencer*, August 27, 2003.

Madison & Washington Parks | Hawthorn (*Crataegus*)

"Parking Strip Tree Selections Listed." *Seattle Sunday Times*, November 24, 1929.

Kim, Gina. "Madison Memoirs." *Seattle Daily Times*, November 12, 2001.

Rochester, Junius. "Seattle Neighborhoods: Madison Park—Thumbnail History." HistoryLink.org, November 16, 2000.

Whitely, Peyton. "Before The Bridge—From 1870 To 1950, Most Eastsiders Who Wanted to Cross Lake Washington Traveled by Ferry." *Seattle Daily Times*, April 16, 1998.

Madison Valley/Denny-Blaine | False Cypress (*Chamaecyparis*)

"The Forest of Washington." *Seattle Daily Times*, June 20, 1900.

Justice, Douglas. "The Untimely Demise of the Lawson Cypress." Pacific Horticulture.

Taylor, Quintard. *The Forging of a Black Community: Seattle's Central District from 1870 through the Civil Rights Era*. Seattle: University of Washington Press, 1994.

Blecha, Peter. "East Madison Street (Seattle)." HistoryLink.org, November 17, 2019.

Henry, Mary T. "Seattle Neighborhoods: Central Area—Thumbnail History." HistoryLink.org, March 10, 2001.

Berger, Maurice. "Documenting the Dynamic Black Community of 1940s Seattle." *New York Times*, March 27, 2018.

Madrona | Arborvitae (*Thuja*)

Rochester, Junius. "Seattle Neighborhoods: Madrona—Thumbnail History." HistoryLink.org, January 10, 1999.

Turner, Nicholas. "Has This Iconic Northwest Tree Reached a Tipping Point?" *Seattle Times*, October 30, 2022.

Wott, John A. "Glimpse into the Past—a Surplus of Cedar." University of Washington Botanic Gardens, November 24, 2015.

"Seattle Black Panther Party History and Memory Project." Seattle Civil Rights & Labor History Project, University of Washington.

Given, Linda Holden. "Black Panther Party Seattle Chapter (1968–1978)." HistoryLink.org, October 16, 2018.

Magnolia | Magnolia (*Magnolia*)

"Where the White Magnolias Bloom." *Seattle Daily Times*, August 11, 1950.

"Strolling Around the Town." *Seattle Daily Times*, June 26, 1936.

"Sweet Magnolia of Tropics Yields Its Perfumed Bloom in Garden of Seattle." *Seattle Daily Times*, July 28, 1927.

"Vandals Destroy Shrubs and Flowers." *Seattle Daily Times*, May 02, 1908.

Fiset, Louis. "Seattle Neighborhoods: Magnolia—Thumbnail History." HistoryLink.org, May 30, 2001.

Eaton, Jeremy. "City, Community Work to Save Magnolia Blvd. Landscape." *Queen Anne & Magnolia News*, March 3, 2014.

"A Timeline of Magnolia Boulevard." Magnolia Historical Society.

Wooton, Monica. "Snapshot in Time: Magnolia Boulevard—The Not So Secret and Secret History Revealed." Magnolia Historical Society, March 2, 2014.

"Indians' Encampment Blocked." *Seattle Daily Times*, September 1970.

Carson, Jerry. "Indians Face Court Battle Over Puyallup Fishing." *Seattle Daily Times*, September 1970.

Wilma, David. "Tacoma Police Arrest 60 Persons at a Fish-In on September 9, 1970." HistoryLink.org: August 25, 2000

Chrisman, Gabriel. "The Fish-in Protests at Franks Landing." University of Washington: The Seattle Civil Rights & Labor History Project, 2008.

Maple Leaf | Poplar (*Populus*)
Krishnan, Sonia. "Diseased, Disruptive Trees Getting the Ax." *Seattle Times*, August 29, 2007.

"Nader Loses Bid for Smoking Ban." *Seattle Times*, August 18, 1970.

Pallini, Thomas. "It's been 20 years since smoking was completely banned on all US flights. Here's how smoking on planes went from normal to banned." *Business Insider*, March 8, 2020.

Wilma, David. "Seattle Neighborhoods: Maple Leaf—Thumbnail History." HistoryLink.org, June 20, 2001.

Mount Baker | Linden (*Tilia*)
Solly, Cecil. "Trees for Parking-Strip Use Should Be Chosen Carefully." *Seattle Daily Times*, December 9, 1962.

Berger, Knute. "In a Time of Rampant Change, an Enduring Mount Baker Makes History." *Crosscut*, November 23, 2018.

Rochester, Junius. "Seattle Neighborhoods: Mount Baker—Thumbnail History." HistoryLink.org, July 23, 2001.

Tenche-Constantinescu, Alina-Maria, et al. "The Symbolism of the Linden Tree." *Journal of Horticulture, Forestry and Biotechnology* 19, no. 2, 2015.

Tobin, Caroline. "Mount Baker Historic Context." City of Seattle, May 2004.

Phinney Ridge | Cedar (*Cedrus*)
Bigelow, John. "Prize Winners Along the Times' 1949 Christmas Trail." *Seattle Daily Times*, December 28, 1949.

"Tree Decoration Proves Popular Over Wide Area." *Seattle Daily Times*, December 28, 1928.

"Winning Trees." *Seattle Daily Times*, December 31, 1947.

"Evergreen Club Plans Lane of Trees at Naval Airbase." *Seattle Daily Times*, May 18, 1930.

"Forest to Mark Tribute." *Seattle Daily Times*, June 28, 1931.

"Interest Over Tree Way Grows." *Seattle Daily Times*, June 6, 1930.

"Mrs. Smith, 73, Dies." *Seattle Times*, August 29, 2007.

Fiset, Louis. "Seattle Neighborhoods: Phinney—Thumbnail History." HistoryLink.org, August 29, 2001.

"First-to-Go Seattle Draft Men Universally Fatalistic About Call." *Seattle Daily Times*, July 9, 1950.

Queen Anne (Northwest) | Birch (*Betula*)
Mapes, Lynda V. "From Mountain Forests to City Parks, Trees are Stressed and Dying." *Seattle Times*, August 6, 2016.

Rule, Misty Shock. "More Dying Birch Trees Removed." University of Washington, September 13, 2018.

Gardner, Nancy. "What's Killing the Birch Trees?" University of Washington, October 10, 2022.

Farrow, Roy. "November 2016 Plant Profile: *Betula nigra*." *University of Washington Botanic Gardens* (blog), October 27, 2016.

Nelson, Glenn. "Seattle's Trees Are Dying. Blame the Beetles." *Crosscut*, September 18, 2019.

McNichols, Joshua. "Some Seattle Trees Have Had It with These Dry Summers." *KUOW*, August 20, 2018.

Queen Anne (Southwest) | Beech (*Fagus*)
"The Heritage Tree Program." PlantAmnesty.org.

Wilma, David. "Seattle Neighborhoods: Queen Anne Hill—Thumbnail History." HistoryLink.org, June 28, 2011.

Lentz, Florence K. "Queen Anne Historical Statement." Seattle Department of Neighborhoods, October 2005.

"Washington Tree Named in Park Fete." *Seattle Daily Times*, July 22, 1931.

"Work Is Role Of Patriotic Club in State." *Seattle Daily Times*, July 15, 1934.

"Washington Tree At Volunteer Dedication." *Seattle Daily Times*, July 26, 1931.

Ravenna | Hemlock (*Tsuga*)

Wilma, David. "Seattle Neighborhoods: Ravenna–Roosevelt—Thumbnail History." HistoryLink.org, August 20, 2001.

Blecha, Peter. "Ravenna Park (Seattle)." HistoryLink.org, January 23, 2011.

McDonald, Lucy. "Phenomenal Seeding in Willapa Hemlock Stand." *Seattle Daily Times*, August 27, 1950.

Higman, Harry W. "Lovely Hemlock Tree Wears Mossy Beards." *Seattle Daily Times*, November 9, 1958.

Williams, David B. "Seattle Parks Department Cuts Down Huge Ravenna Park Trees in the Mid-1920s." HistoryLink.org, March 31, 2010.

Arnst, Albert. "3-Time Forest Harvest." *Seattle Daily Times*, August 17, 1947.

"Seeing the Forest for the Trees: Placing Washington's Forests in Historical Context." Center for the Study of the Pacific Northwest.

Bass, Kayley. "The Hidden History of Western Washington Logging Camps: St. Paul and Tacoma Lumber Company's Camp #5 ca. 1934–1947." Central Washington University, Summer 2007.

"Trees Everywhere, But Nary a One That's Official." *Seattle Daily Times*, March 10, 1946.

"One More Vote For Red Cedar As State Tree." *Seattle Daily Times*, April 10, 1946.

"Keep Out of This, Oregon." *Seattle Daily Times*, April 14, 1946.

Hillaire, Joseph R. "Times Readers Have Their Say." *Seattle Daily Times*, April 21, 1946.

"Staff to Cut Own Logs For Scarce Paper." *Seattle Daily Times*, May 28, 1946.

"Official Tree Choice in Laps Of Legislators." *Seattle Daily Times*, February 12, 1947.

Roanoke | Elm (*Ulmus*)

Collins, Alf. "Odd Parcels." *Seattle Daily Times*, January 21, 1973.

Arksey, Laura. "Spokane's Champion and Historic Trees." HistoryLink.org, February 7, 2012.

Becker, Paula. "Seattle Neighborhoods: Portage Bay-Roanoke-North Capitol Hill—Thumbnail History." HistoryLink.org, December 25, 2012.

Ketcherside, Rob. "Roanoke Park and Seattle's Broadway Streetcar." *Ba-kground* (blog), June 5, 2014.

"Roanoke Park." Friends of Seattle's Olmsted Parks.

O'Connor, Erin. "National Register of Historic Places Registration Form: Roanoke Historic District." US Department of the Interior, June 17, 2009.

Nelson, Catherine. "June 2018 Plant Profile: Finding the Story of Our George Washington Elm." *University of Washington Botanic Gardens* (blog), May 31, 2018.

Halberg, Alicia. "George Washington Tree." *University of Washington* (blog), October 7, 2016.

Griffin, Tom. "Washington Elm is a Campus Landmark with a Storied History." *University of Washington Magazine*, September 2003.

"An Elm Tree in Seattle History." *Wedgwood in Seattle History*, July 8, 2022.

"Scion of the Washington Elm—Seattle, WA." Washington Historical Marketers, Waymarking.com, April 4, 2017.

King, Seth S. "Dutch Elm Disease Spreads Westward." September 7, 1971.

"National Elm Trial at WSU Puyallup." Washington State University.

Egge, Rose. "Dutch Elm Disease Infecting Trees." *Westside Seattle*, September 15, 2008.

Maples, Lynda V. "Centenarian Elm Falls in Seattle Park, Closing a Chapter of History." *Seattle Times*, January 13, 2018.

Brunner, Jim. "Tree Owners Warned about Dutch Elm Disease." *Seattle Times*, 2008.

South Park | Catalpa (*Catalpa*)

"'City Beautiful' Campaign Begins for South Park." *Seattle Daily Times*, March 23, 1930.

Solly, Cecil. "Catalpas Provide Good Mottled Shade." *Seattle Daily Times*, October 22, 1961.

"Horrifying Hint," editorial. *Seattle Daily Times*, November 11, 1942.

Wilma, David. "Seattle Neighborhoods: South Park—Thumbnail History." HistoryLink.org, February 16, 2001.

Veith, Thomas. "History of South Park." Seattle Historic Preservation Program, City of Seattle Department of Neighborhoods, 2009.

"Time for Planting Trees Is at Hand." *Seattle Daily Times*, March 12, 1911.

University District | Horse Chestnut (*Aesculus*)

Martin, Genna, and Zosha Millman. "Then and Now: The University District through the Ages." *Seattle Post-Intelligencer*, August 26, 2019.

Dorpat, Paul. "Seattle Neighborhoods: University District—Thumbnail History." HistoryLink.org, June 16, 2001.

Kreisnan, Lawrence. "Frat Row." *Seattle Post-Intelligencer*, February 12, 1989.

Holtz, Jackson. "UW's 2022 Entering Class Is Largest and Most Diverse." University of Washington, news release, October 14, 2022.

Smith, Alison Jean. "Shiga's Imports Reflects on 67 Years." *The Daily*, April 18, 2023.

Shiotani, Yuki. "History of the Cherry Trees in Liberal Arts Quadrangle at the University of Washington." University of Washington thesis, 2018, 30–33.

Stevens, Jeff. "August 11, 1969: The Ave Riots." *Radical Seattle Remembers* (blog), August 11, 2014.

Berger, Knute. "A Short, Violent History of Puget Sound Uprisings, Protests and Riots." *Crosscut*, June 5, 2020.

"Strolling Around the Town: Tulip Takes Its Time." *Seattle Daily Times*, June 26, 1950.

Wallingford | Firs (*Abies* and *Pseudotsuga*)

Arnst, Albert. "3-Time Forest Harvest." *Seattle Daily Times*, August 17, 1947.

Palmer, Mary. "Trees Offer Much But Ask Little." *Seattle Daily Times*, May 8, 1966.

Dougherty, Phil. "Northgate Center Lights the World's Tallest Christmas Tree." HistoryLink.org, November 26, 2021.

Dorpat, Paul. "Seattle Neighborhoods: Wallingford—Thumbnail History." HistoryLink.org, July 24, 2001.

"Local History Features." Historic Wallingford.

Dietrich, William. "Douglas Fir, Then and Now." *Seattle Times*, March 19, 2000.

Veith, Thomas. "A Preliminary Sketch of Wallingford's History 1855–1985." Seattle Department of Neighborhoods, 2005.

McNichols, Joshua. "Seattle's Wallingford Neighborhood Gets 'Historic District' Status." *KUOW*, October 14, 2022.

Wedgwood (North) | Spruce (*Picea*)

"The Business District of Wedgwood, Then and Now." *Wedgwood in Seattle History* (blog), October 10, 2019.

"How Wedgwood Came into the City Limits of Seattle." *Wedgwood in Seattle History* (blog), August 20, 2012.

"More Forests Needed By State." *Seattle Daily Times*, December 14, 1928.

"Little Spruce to Grow Into Christmas Model." *Seattle Daily Times*, December 18, 1928.

"Evergreen—All but Parking Strips." *Seattle Daily Times*, July 20, 1960.

"The Scout Camp in Wedgwood." *Wedgwood in Seattle* (blog), February 27, 2012.

King, Warren. "Coinless Telephone Makes Its Debut in Seattle." *Seattle Daily Times*, July 7, 1979.

Wilma, David. "Seattle Neighborhoods: Wedgwood—Thumbnail History." HistoryLink.org, June 24, 2001.

Wedgwood (South) | Oak (*Quercus*)

Guzzo, Louis R. "Art Commission OKs Street Tree Program." *Seattle Daily Times*, November 15, 1957.

Hume, Ed. "It's Oaky-Dokey—If You've Got Enough Room." *Seattle Daily Times*, November 2, 1977.

Malcolm, Patrick A. "History of Oak Trees, *Quercus Sp.*" *Pioneer Thinking*, n.d.

O'Brien, Kirsten. "Real Estate Profile: Wedgwood Homes." *Seattle Post-Intelligencer*, May 13, 2015.

West Seattle | Yew (*Taxus*)

"West Seattle." Seattle Municipal Archive.

Tate, Cassandra. "Seattle Neighborhoods: West Seattle—Thumbnail History." HistoryLink.org, July 8, 2001.

Index

Note: Page numbers in *italic* refer to illustrations.

About the Author

Taha Ebrahimi was born and raised in Seattle where she returned after spending fifteen years on the East Coast. During the creation of this book, she was director of a free data visualization platform called Tableau Public. Her writing has appeared in *Creative Nonfiction*, *Crosscut*, the *Seattle Times*, and numerous anthologies, and she is the recipient of awards from the Pacific Northwest Writers' Association, the Mid-Atlantic Arts Foundation, and the Thomas J. Watson Foundation. She serves as a member of the council for Historic Seattle as well as the board for the Cal Anderson Park Alliance. This is her first book.